GUIDE TO
California Wines

GUIDE TO
California Wines

BY JOHN MELVILLE

REVISED BY JEFFERSON MORGAN

FIFTH EDITION

A Sunrise Book
E. P. DUTTON & CO., INC.
New York

FIFTH EDITION

10 9 8 7 6 5 4 3 2 1

Published simultaneously in Canada by Clarke, Irwin & Company Limited, Toronto and Vancouver
ISBN: 0-87690-176-3
Dutton-Sunrise, Inc., a subsidiary of E. P. Dutton & Co., Inc.

Library of Congress Cataloging in Publication Data
Melville, John, 1903–
    Guide to California wines.

    "A Sunrise book."
    1. Wine and wine making—California. I. Morgan, Jefferson. II. Title.
TP557.M4   1975   641.2'2'09794   75-12065

To the memory

of

Joseph Henry Jackson

who first made this book possible

and

To the memory

of

James Pomeroy Howe

foreign correspondent, bon vivant,
winemaker, pigeon raiser, turkey smoker
and God knows what else, who encouraged
its revision

ACKNOWLEDGMENTS
TO THE FIFTH EDITION

Unfortunately, there isn't room here to list the countless people who should be thanked for their help and encouragement through the various revisions of this book. They know who they are, and I hope they will again accept my gratitude. A few, however, deserve special thanks:

—*A. Dinsmoor Webb* and *James F. Guymon*, Professors of Enology, and *Harold P. Olmo*, Professor of Viticulture at the University of California, Davis, for carefully checking and rechecking Part I of the *Guide* over the years and suggesting changes and additions which we hope we have faithfully incorporated;

—California's *winemakers, vineyard owners* and others in and around the wine industry who have responded to our many questions;

—My wife, *Jinx*, without whom I couldn't do anything.

Jefferson Morgan

PREFACE
TO THE FIFTH EDITION

AT THE TIME of his death, John Melville was planning another revision of this *Guide*. His passing and the popularity of the second edition postponed it. However, as wineries went out of existence and others were founded, and as personalities and products changed, it became obvious a completely updated version was overdue. The job was undertaken in 1968 on assignment from the publisher, again in 1971, and once again in 1976.

Baron John Melville Van-Carnbee, who simplified his name for the purposes of authorship, was something of a crusader who wanted every man and woman in America to know the delights of California wines. It was an ambitious mission, but one which he undertook with gusto.

Born at The Hague, the son of a Dutch diplomat, John Melville gained his discerning appreciation of fine wines in his father's cellar. He became a Doctor of International Law, lecturer and author of a work on social economics. During World War II he fought with the infantry and air forces of the Free Netherlands Army, ending up as a lieutenant colonel, and was posted to Washington by his government between 1945 and 1950.

It was after that he moved to Carmel and began writing this book, a task he believed would be completed in a year. It actually took four to compile the basic information, although, in his own words, "a pleasanter, more convivial form of literary endeavor would be hard to imagine."

Every effort has been made to preserve the original author's Old World literary style, not an entirely simple chore in view of his diverse linguistic background. We hope we have been successful.

We also have retained the original author's order of battle. Part I of this volume describes various kinds of wine produced in California, grouped according to type. Part II deals with some notable or interesting wineries and personalities involved in winemaking. Part III covers, perhaps inadequately, the serving of wine, wineglasses, a list of outstanding California wines and finally a listing of wineries open to the public.

In the second edition John Melville warned that in spite of the help and assistance of those persons and organizations mentioned in the acknowledgments, errors of fact or judgment will undoubtedly have crept into the text. We repeat his invitation for correspondence to correct them.

Oakland, California

CONTENTS

Part Two

DRAWINGS

CHARTS

CALIFORNIA VINES AND WINES

$\mathscr{C}$ALIFORNIA WINES are produced from vines imported from Europe or from neighboring regions, and belonging to the Old World *Vitis vinifera* species of grapes.

The art of wine making was brought to California by the Spaniards. From Mexico wine growing spread northward to Baja California and finally to what was then known as Alta California. According to tradition, Padre Junipero Serra, of Mission fame, brought the first vines from Baja California and planted them at Mission San Diego in or about 1769. The Franciscan Fathers planted vines near the various Missions they established along their Camino Real stretching northward to Sonoma. The oldest California winery is to be found at Mission San Gabriel, where the famed Trinity Vine, planted around 1775, flourished for over a century and a half. It was from San Gabriel that settlers set forth one day to establish the Pueblo which was to become the city of Los Angeles.

The Mission Fathers planted what became known as the Mission grape, popular for long and still used today, mainly in the production of dessert wines.

The first layman wine grower of record was Governor Pedro Fages, who planted a vineyard along with his orchards in 1783, not far from his residence in Monterey, Alta California. Dona Marcelina

Felix Dominguez, the first known woman wine grower of California, planted, in the early eighteen hundreds, at Montecito near Santa
Barbara, a fabulous vine which was to bear in good years some four
tons of grapes. Known as *La Vieja de la Parra Grande,* or "The Old
Lady of the Grapevine," she was said to be 105 years old when she
died in 1865.

For a time Los Angeles led the rest of California in wine growing.
There Joseph Chapman, an early immigrant, is conceded to have
been the first viticulturist. He is far overshadowed in fame by Jean
Louis Vignes, a native of the Bordeaux region in France and the
possessor of a most appropriate name. By 1843 his celebrated Aliso
Vineyard, in the heart of what is now downtown Los Angeles and
named after a large sycamore which dominated the entrance to his
property, covered over a hundred acres. Don Louis del Aliso, as he
became known, was the first to import choice vines from Europe
and to realize the great future of California wines, produced from
these varieties. Many of his relatives followed him from France, including Pierre Sanssevain, who became a well-known grower in his
own right.

In the northern region the first great wine growing pioneer was
General Mariano Guadalupe Vallejo. Born in Monterey of Castilian
descent he rose to prominence at an early age, becoming closely
identified with the Mexican and early American history of California
and especially with that of Sonoma, where he resided for many years.
He was a great gentleman, farmer, soldier and philosopher. He accepted the "manifest destiny" whereby Alta California, in its own
interest and by the force of circumstances, was to become part of
the United States. In June 1846 a company of Americans ran up the
Bear Flag in the plaza of Sonoma and soon afterward the American
Army raised the flag of the United States. Vallejo, in spite of a brief
incarceration by the overly patriotic Bears, accepted the new regime.
He continued to devote himself to his agricultural pursuits and to
aid immigrant Yankees to settle in the newly opened region. He was
the first non-missionary wine grower in the Sonoma Valley and

dominated the viticultural scene there for many years, until the advent of Haraszthy.

Colonel Agoston Haraszthy is often referred to as "the father of California's modern wine industry." It is greatly owing to his genius that a sound and lasting basis was created for the state's viticulture. It is a pleasing thought that the wine growing estate near Sonoma, which Haraszthy called Buena Vista and made famous, is in operation today. It is there that some of the story of this colorful California wine growing pioneer will be found.

California wineries have a long and proud tradition. Many of the better-known enterprises flourishing today were founded in the nineteenth century, some still being run by members of the founding family. Their listing by county and in approximate chronological order, according to the owners' claims, presents an intriguing historical and geographical picture.

In 1849, or earlier, the vineyards in San Benito County now known as Valliant Vineyards were started by Theophile Vaché. In Santa Clara, Almadén, Paul Masson and Martin Ray are the successors to wine making traditions begun in 1852. In the same county Mirassou Vineyards originated a year later, some four years earlier than Buena Vista in Sonoma. The early sixties saw the beginnings of Charles Krug in Napa and of Schramsberg. Dating back to the seventies are Beringer Brothers in Napa, and Inglenook in Napa.

In the eighties a galaxy of famous wineries was founded, including Italian Swiss Colony and Korbel in Sonoma, Mt. La Salle (The Christian Brothers) in Napa, Brookside Vineyard Company of Guasti, Cresta Blanca, Wente and Concannon in Alameda, Italian Vineyards Company (I.V.C.) in San Bernardino (now owned by the Guild Wine Company), California Wine Association in San Francisco, Digardi in Contra Costa, Petri in San Joaquin, Ruby Hill in Alameda, the Novitiate of Los Gatos in Santa Clara and Bisceglia Brothers in Fresno.

The nineties witnessed the foundings of Roma, now of Fresno, of

San Martin in Santa Clara and of Foppiano, in Sonoma. In 1900 the foundations were laid for Beaulieu in Napa.

Since then many other wineries, great and small, have risen to establish noteworthy wine making traditions of their own.

Prohibition dealt a severe blow to American viticulture in general and that of California in particular. It was a senseless attack, as Prohibition has never led the way to moderation and encroaches deeply on man's freedom of judgment. A substantial part of California's vineyard acreage was maintained for the production of wines for sacramental and medicinal purposes and for supplying grapes to home wine makers, as allowed by the dry laws. Other vineyards were turned over to the cultivation of table grapes and to the manufacture of grape juice.

After Repeal the California wine industry was rebuilt on a sound basis with the State Department of Public Health and the federal government becoming joint guardians for the maintenance of standards as to the identity and labeling of wines.

In the decades after Repeal, California's winemakers labored hard and long to breathe life back into an industry that virtually had been eliminated by the tyranny of Prohibition. Per capita consumption of table wine in America rose slowly, agonizingly, from almost nothing until in the early sixties it had reached nearly one gallon per year per person (not much of a record compared with 30 times that in France and Italy).

Then came an explosion of consumption, triggered partly by an increase in disposable income, partly by industry promotion, but especially by the improvement in quality of California wines. There were two predictable results: corporate takeovers of existing well-known wineries and tremendous vineyard expansion. Prior to 1964 there were 104,174 acres planted to wine grapes in California, out of total grape acreage of 386,754 (including raisins and table varieties). By 1974 there were more than 290,000 acres of wine grapes, most of them planted within the past few years. The 1974 crop was a staggering 3,750,000 tons (by comparison only 125,000 tons of grapes were crushed for wine in New York State in 1973). Total California vineyard acreage was over 610,000, and despite a slowdown in the growth of wine sales and a reduction of from 25 to 50% in grape prices, additional planting was going ahead. As an example of the boom, Monterey County had 1,924 bearing acres of wine grapes in 1972. Two years later there were 7,000 acres producing, most planted to expensive premium varietals, with 37,000 acres more already planted for future harvesting.

During this same period in the late sixties and early seventies—a time winemaster Alexis Lichine has called "the period of euphoria"—corporate giants attracted by visions of huge profits began taking over some of California's oldest and most respected wineries. For instance, Heublein Inc. acquired Beaulieu Vineyard as well as United Vintners, the successor to the Petri empire which already had purchased Italian Swiss Colony and Inglenook; Nestle became the proprietor of Beringer Bros.; the Schlitz brewing people acquired Geyser Peak in Healdsburg and the old Nervo Winery nearby; Scottish & Newcastle Importers Co. purchased Simi Winery in the same region; the Pillsbury milling company took over and greatly expanded Souverain. These and other diversified interests joined corporations such as National Distillers and Chemical Corp., already owner of Almaden, and the House of Seagram, which had acquired Paul Masson Vineyards.

Other, less institutional investors were entranced with the idea of becoming vignerons, and in the first half of the seventies literally dozens of small new wineries, most dedicated to the making of premium, often expensive wines, came on the scene.

Inflation and depression, two economic ills not often experienced simultaneously, struck California's wine industry as it did many others, and grape prices, artificially high in previous years, plunged during the 1974 harvest. Growers who had enjoyed several years of unprecedented prosperity spoke darkly of building their own cooperative winery on the North Coast to make wine and withhold it from the market until prices improved.

But, as Thomas Tusser said in the sixteenth century, "It is an ill wind that turns none to good." The beneficiary of overplanting and overproduction eventually could be the consumer. Perhaps not lower, but at least stable prices for wine should result. The ill-advised speculators probably will be shaken out, leaving the field to those willing on occasion to sacrifice profit in order to make good wine. And although sales in the mid-seventies were sluggish compared with previous years, they continued to inch up because of what had attracted American consumers in the first place: the continual improvement in quality that has earned California wines their international reputation.

California is responsible for roughly 80 per cent of the wine produced in the United States, and for about 75 per cent of that consumed in this country. Ten years ago, 75 per cent of California's production consisted of aperitif and dessert wines, compared with less than half today. The balance is mainly table and sparkling or carbonated wines. Although exact figures are hard to come by, it has been estimated that about four-fifths of California table wines are red (including rosés), and about one-fifth white.

The climate and soil of California are particularly well suited to the vines of the *Vitis vinifera* family. Beginning with the days of Jean Louis Vignes and of Agoston Haraszthy, practically every variety of these vines has been planted in California, many of them with great success. By the alchemy of local conditions they yield wines which often differ in character from those produced in their original environments. California wines, while often similar or identical in name to European types, should always be considered on their own merits, but comparisons, it seems, are often inevitable.

The same grapes also develop differently in the various regions and climates of California. Maturity is slow in cooler areas. White grapes retain more acid and develop less sweetness, while dark grapes attain the maximum coloring matter in their skins. These regions are best suited for the production of dry table wines and of sparkling wines of quality. Under warmer conditions grapes develop less acid and a greater sugar content. Such zones are better adapted to the production of dessert wines.

It is known exactly to which localities each grape variety is best suited or whether its cultivation should be avoided altogether. Such studies and recommendations are among the important functions of the Department of Viticulture and Enology of the University of California's College of Agriculture at Davis in Yolo County and of a similar department at Fresno State College.

Full recognition must be given to a great line of university figures who have wisely guided California's viticulture and are seeking constant improvement. First of that line was the famed Dean Hilgard who was succeeded by Bioletti, or the great Bioletti as he is often referred to. Both have long since passed on, to supervise, it may be hoped, the heavenly vineyards. Their places were taken by such men, professors of viticulture or enology, as Winkler, Amerine, Olmo, Singleton, Berg, Guymon, Kunkee, Webb, Cook, Lider, Weaver, Kliewer, Nelson and the late W. V. Cruess, familiar figures to all members of the wine industry.

Other researchers, best known among them Dr. Salvatore Lucia, Professor Emeritus of Preventive Medicine at the University of California Medical Center in San Francisco, have rediscovered wine's nutritional and medicinal benefits. They have learned that it is a complex food, useful as a dietary supplement or tranquilizer for patients afflicted with a variety of ailments.

Wine growing and wine production are important and fundamental parts of California's agriculture. There are many more farmergrowers than producers. The interests of both should be adequately protected. Wine making is also a business, subject to the hazards of weather and diseases, to fluctuating grape prices, and to high labor costs. It is at the same time an art, requiring the skill, patience, and devotion of experts.

Fine wines are produced from the better wine grapes, but the latter are often sparse yielders. Standard wines are the product of the more heavily yielding vines of lesser quality. Inferior wines are not infrequently made with table grapes.

Wines produced from the finest grapes naturally will command a higher price. For such wines the name on the label of an outstanding wine grower is helpful as a guarantee of quality. If a sound standard quality wine is sought at a lower price, then the name of a volume producer of a nationally distributed brand should be looked for. These wines are advertised widely and provide good value for the money.

California wine growers often produce, bottle and market wines of many different types, growing some grapes themselves and buying the rest from growers in the neighborhood or from other districts. It is customary for a large producer to market a variety of table wines as well as aperitif and dessert wines and often sparkling wines as well. One reason for this custom is that many different varieties of grapes flourish in the same vicinity; vines which are strangers or even rivals in Europe become friendly neighbors in California. Another, and very potent, reason is that it is much more profitable to market a large variety of wines than otherwise. Only a few California wineries produce wines only from grapes grown in their own vineyards. Most of them buy outside grapes as needed and many bottle wines they do not produce themselves in order to complete the selection of wines they want to market. It must be stressed that the fact that a wine is actually produced at a specific winery from homegrown grapes only can never be as important as the quality of the wine itself, backed by the reputation of the winery which either produces or markets it.

Part One

I

CALIFORNIA TABLE WINES

THE TABLE WINES of California can best be classified according to color; red, white or rosé, and as to whether they are *generic* or *varietal.*

By *generic* is meant a wine called after its European prototype which it resembles, more or less. The names are familiar, easy to pronounce and are met with the world over. In California the best known of such table wines are burgundy, claret and chianti in the reds, sauterne, chablis and rhine in the whites, and vin rosé meaning pink wine.

By *varietal* is meant a wine named after a particular *variety of grape,* from which it is principally or exclusively produced and having the easily recognizable taste characteristics of the variety. The best known California varietal red table wines are Cabernet Sauvignon, Zinfandel, Pinot Noir and Gamay. In the whites they are: Sauvignon Blanc and Semillon; Chardonnay, Pinot Blanc and Chenin Blanc; White Riesling, Traminer, Sylvaner and Grey Riesling. In the rosés they are Grenache Rosé, Gamay Rosé and Cabernet Rosé. These are all names to remember if one wishes to serve the more distinctive and finer table wines of California.

In marketing a table wine with a generic name the producer either tries to approximate the European wine type after which it is called or he simply uses the name in response to public demand. The public insists on burgundy and sauterne. The producers, to stay in business, must comply.

The trend towards varietal table wines is increasing as the public becomes more particular as to quality and flavor. The laws are strict and a wine can—or should be—called after a grape *only* if 51% or more of the wine is produced from the grape. A varietal wine should also possess the distinctive color, aroma and flavor of the particular grape. These qualities should be easily recognizable and not only by the experts. There is little point in producing a varietal wine just for the sake of the name.

Some fine California table wines are produced from a careful blending of choice grape varieties, each lending its own character to the final product. The French Bordeaux wines, both red and white, are usually blended in this manner. There is a place in California for blends as well as for the varietals, straight or otherwise.

Vintage years matter less in California than in France and Germany where temperatures, affecting the grape harvests and the resulting wines, vary considerably. Even so, some years in California are more favorable than others and there is a definite trend towards marketing the table wines of exceptionally fine vintages at a higher price. This development must be warmly welcomed as is the tendency towards differentiating between superior table wines that mature in different vats. There is that elusive quality in nature that seeks perfection in all things.

Indication of the vintage on a California wine also serves to identify it to the consumer. Vintage charts would only be of real value if made up by each winery for each type of wine produced, indicating the vineyards of origin. Incidentally, if a vintage is mentioned on the label, the wine must, by law, have been produced 95% in the year indicated.

Which are the finest California table wines?

The answer involves three separate factors: the grapes from which the wines are made, the district of origin, and the reputation of the wine grower.

The best table wine grapes yield the finest wines. It is therefore useful to be familiar with these grapes after which the finer varietals are named.

The superior table wine grapes flourish the best in the cooler climatic zones, where they grow and mature "the hard way." For that reason the finest California table wines hail from the northern coastal counties, notably in the counties or valleys of *Napa, Sonoma, Livermore, Santa Clara, Santa Cruz, San Benito* and *Monterey*.

These are the "appellations of origin" to look for on the label when desiring the best. Any such appellation means, by law, that the wine has been produced from grapes grown and fermented at least 75% in the area designated.

Premium table wines are also produced in other northern sections as in the counties of Mendocino, Solano and Contra Costa. There has been a resurgence of winegrowing in the Mother Lode counties of the Sierra foothills.

Separate mention must be made of the red table wines produced in the Cucamonga district of San Bernardino County in Southern California. Many of these wines carry the *Cucamonga* appellation of origin on the label.

The ultimate guarantee of quality for any wine is the reputation of the grower or producer.

CHART OF THE MORE PROMINENT CALIFORNIA RED TABLE WINES

Varietals	Generics
CABERNET SAUVIGNON	Claret
PINOT NOIR	Burgundy
GAMAY	
ZINFANDEL	
BARBERA	Chianti
GRIGNOLINO	Vino Rosso
PETITE SIRAH	

II

CALIFORNIA RED TABLE WINES

A. Varietals

CABERNET SAUVIGNON (Ca-berr-nay′ So-vee-nyon′)

THE CABERNET SAUVIGNON, to use its full and proper name, is the premier claret grape of the world. It is mainly responsible for the superb character and flavor of the celebrated château-bottled and other clarets of the Bordeaux region in France.

In California the Cabernet Sauvignon grape can yield, in the northern coastal region, altogether superior wines. Napa, Santa Clara, Santa Cruz and Sonoma counties produce the finest, some of which are great wines anywhere under the sun.

The finest Cabernet Sauvignons are produced from considerably more than the legal minimum of 51% of grapes of that name as the wine will not stand much blending without loss of character. The best have a deep ruby color, an expansive bouquet and a remarkable flavor, easy to recognize and appreciate. When young they possess a dryness and aromatic pungency that smooth out with age to a rich mellowness. A common mistake is to serve them at a temperature cooler than the average room. At room temperature their inherent tartness will dissolve into their rightful soft and mellow flavor.

There is a wide range of Cabernet Sauvignons, depending on the location of the vineyard, the grower, the age, and even the vat in which the wine matured.

When one desires the best "claret type" California can produce, a fine Cabernet Sauvignon is the wine to buy.

CABERNET

A wine, labeled simply Cabernet, can be one of very different things and the term is therefore confusing.

It could be made mainly of Cabernet Sauvignon grapes (see above) and should then properly so have been named.

It could be made principally from the Ruby Cabernet grape (see below) in which case it would better have been labeled by its own name.

It could be made from a blend of various grapes with the Cabernet name. The label may tell the story or it may not.

This writer, for one, is for abolishing the term entirely.

RUBY CABERNET

A fairly new varietal in the red table wine field. Propagated by the Agricultural Experiment Station of the University of California, the vine is a hybrid of the Cabernet Sauvignon and of the Carignane grapes from a cross made in 1936 which first fruited in 1940. Purpose of the cross was to combine the outstanding character of the Cabernet Sauvignon with the productivity of the Carignane in an attempt to combine high quality and yielding ability in the same variety.

The color of Ruby Cabernet is the same as that of its august parent, Cabernet Sauvignon. Its aroma and flavor are superior in the warmer regions.

Ruby Cabernet rates as a red table wine of higher than average quality. The wine is varietally produced in a number of northern coastal and San Joaquin Valley counties.

ZINFANDEL

The leading red wine grape of California in acreage, production and originality.

Its origin is uncertain. The best known theory was that the wine was first imported to California by Colonel Agoston Haraszthy, who planted these vines at his Buena Vista estate near Sonoma where they flourished and made viticultural history.

Zinfandel varies considerably in quality and character, the best coming from the coastal counties. It can be a wine of peculiar charm, fruity, zestful and aromatic with a raspberry like flavor. It is essentially Californian in type and has the great advantage of being remarkably inexpensive.

If price conscious and still wanting a varietal red table wine, a good Zinfandel is the wine to look for.

PINOT NOIR (Pee'-no Nwahr)

This is the famous grape that yields the finest of the Red Burgundies of France and the "Blanc de noir" wines from which most of the unblended French Champagnes are produced.

In California the Pinot noir grape* produces wines that can be superb in aroma and flavor, harmonious, soft, smooth and velvety. One hundred % Pinot Noir in California is almost always light in color as the grape does not carry much pigment so blending to darken color is nearly standard practice.

Napa, Santa Clara and Sonoma counties originate the best. The vine, however, is difficult to cultivate and the wine itself is as difficult to produce properly. Availability of the true Pinot Noir wine is limited and wine, so labeled, varies greatly in quality. It can never be cheap if genuine.

If one desires the highest quality California red burgundy type then a truly fine Pinot Noir is the wine to purchase.

GAMAY BEAUJOLAIS (Ga-may' Bo-zho-lay') and GAMAY

The Gamay is the grape that made the Beaujolais wines of France famous and is responsible for their gay and fruity character.

---

* Pinot Noir is the correct spelling for the *wine* and Pinot noir for the *grape*. This principle applies to all wines and grapes where the name is followed by an adjective.

In California the Gamay produces a light colored, lively and fruity wine with a delicate flavor.

There are many varieties of the Gamay vine, all similar, more or less. Gamay Beaujolais is produced in Santa Clara and San Benito Counties, while the Napa County variety is always labeled simply as Gamay.

It may be noted that Gamay, like Beaujolais in France, is often served at cellar temperature.

RED PINOT (Pinot St. George)

There is no grape by the name of Red Pinot. The term, however, has won limited acceptance as a red table wine, produced from the Pinot St. George grape, the name under which the wine itself should also be known.

Pinot St. George, no relation to the pinot family but a variety from the south of France, produces a wine of its own distinctive charm, soft, fruity and fragrant. It is produced only in the Napa Valley.

PETITE SIRAH (Pet-eet Sear-ah)

An ancient *vinifera* grape, said to have been brought by the Crusaders from the Middle East to the Rhone Valley of France, where it produces the red wines of Hermitage. It was transplanted to California and is widely grown. A few wineries such as Concannon Vineyards in Livermore bottle Petite Sirah as red varietal, although most use it as a blending wine.

BARBERA

A native of Piedmont, Italy, which has done very well in California. The grape yields a big, rugged, fullbodied, richly colored and very pleasant wine with plenty of flavor and tang which yet can be quite soft to the palate. It is characterized by high acidity which it retains very well. Notable Barberas are produced in Sonoma and Alameda counties.

GRIGNOLINO

Another native of Piedmont producing in California a wine with an original and popular appeal. Its fragrant bouquet is said to remind one of strawberries and its orange-red color is typical and unique. It is sometimes bottled, on account of its light color, as Grignolino Rosé. The best known Grignolinos are produced in Cucamonga and in Napa.

Charbono

Also said to originate in Piedmont, this grape produces a deep-colored, soft and heavy bodied wine.

Calzin

A red grape introduced in 1958 by the University of California.

Royalty and Rubired

Two red varieties developed at Davis by University of California scientists. Both have high color and are useful as blending wines or for making California port. At least one winery has begun marketing Royalty as a varietal table wine.

B. GENERICS

RED TABLE WINE

A wine which has become increasingly popular and is often of very good quality, selling in the medium price range. It makes no pretenses and can be produced from a wide variety of grapes. It seems to be taking the place of Claret and is usually of better quality than the latter.

CLARET

Usually a standard quality wine of no particular distinction, although there are exceptions. Claret used to mean any acceptable red table wine, resembling Red Bourdeaux more or less and usually less. The term seems to be headed for extinction, its place being taken by Red Table Wine (see above) or Burgundy (see below).

BURGUNDY

The most common appellation today for a generic table wine of no particular varietal distinction. It can be pleasant enough and has superseded what once used to be sold as Claret. The public demands Burgundy and gets it.

California wine, labeled Burgundy, varies greatly in quality, and ranges from poor to very good indeed, notably when produced by the better known growers of the northern coastal counties.

CHIANTI

The wine of this name is usually marketed in raffia or straw-covered, bulb shaped bottles. In California Chianti has become a type of wine, ruby red, fruity, earthy, medium tart and rather full-bodied, the best known of which is produced in Asti, Sonoma County.

Note: The four generics described above actually overlap in color, body and other characteristics, the main differences often being the bottle shapes.

VINO ROSSO

This type of table wine, mellow and slightly sweet, is similar to the homemade table wines produced by many people of Italian origin throughout the country. The commercial wine of this type, quite inexpensive, has won wide acceptance, especially in Italian circles. Many growers produce it, labeling it with various Italian names. The original dryness in the wine is often compensated by the addition of a slight amount of port.

CHART OF THE MORE PROMINENT
CALIFORNIA WHITE TABLE WINES

Varietals	Generics
SEMILLON SAUVIGNON BLANC	Sauterne
CHARDONNAY PINOT BLANC CHENIN BLANC FOLLE BLANCHE	Chablis
WHITE RIESLING (JOHANNISBERG) TRAMINER SYLVANER GREY RIESLING	Riesling Rhine Wine Moselle

III

CALIFORNIA WHITE TABLE WINES

A. VARIETALS

SEMILLON (Sem-me-yon')

O NE OF the finest white wine grapes in the world and responsible, together with the Sauvignon Blanc (see below), for the character of the famous Sauternes and Graves wines of France.

Semillon, when produced by a top flight grower in one of the northern coastal counties, ranks as one of the finest California wines of the Sauternes type. It is golden, medium to fullbodied with a rich flavor and a flowery bouquet and ranges from dry to sweet.

Outstanding Semillon wines are produced in the Livermore Valley and other very good ones originate in Napa and Santa Clara.

SAUVIGNON BLANC (So'-vee-nyon Blon)

The principal grape variety used for the production of the white Graves wine of Bordeaux and also important in that of the French Sauternes. Known in France as the Sauvignon, it is called Sauvignon blanc in California to distinguish it clearly from the Sauvignon vert (see below).

Sauvignon Blanc is a high quality wine with a distinctive aromatic

character, fuller in body and heavier than Semillon. Like the latter it
ranges from dry to sweet, the best hailing from the Livermore Valley
with its gravelly soil.

Sauvignon Vert (So'-vee-nyon Vair)

The grape is widely cultivated and much used in blending and in
the production of California Sauterne of average quality.

It is occasionally met with bottled as a varietal type and can be
quite pleasing with its dry character and slight muscat flavor.

French Colombard

Another vigorous producer yielding a wine with a high acid content useful for blending in California chablis and rhine wine types.
As a varietal wine it is dry, light, tart, pale golden with a neutral
flavor.

CHARDONNAY or PINOT CHARDONNAY
(Pee'-no Shar-don-nay)

One of the greatest white wine grapes of all but a sparse yielder. It
is celebrated for producing the finest white burgundies and Chablis
of France as well as being used for French Champagne.

In the cooler northern coastal counties the grape can yield a distinguished wine, golden, fullbodied and fragrant, flavorful and smooth,
reminiscent of still champagne.

The wine is known under both names indicated above which is
confusing and incorrect. It is hoped the first term, which is the right
one, will be agreed upon.

When the finest California wine of the white burgundy or chablis
type is the object, this is the wine to secure, bottled by an outstanding
grower.

PINOT BLANC (Pee'-no Blon)

A grape second only to the Chardonnay in the white burgundy
class. It has made an enviable reputation for itself in California
where it can yield an elegant wine of distinctive aroma and flavor,

smooth and dry, fresh and fruity. Like Chardonnay its favorite California homes are in the Livermore, Napa and Santa Clara valleys.

Some Pinot Blanc is labeled Pinot Blanc Vrai or True Pinot Blanc. This seems unnecessary as the wine is a Pinot Blanc or it isn't. If it isn't, it should be labeled differently.

White Pinot

A misnomer as there is no grape by that name and a very confusing term which, it is hoped, is headed for extinction.

Literally, it is of course the translation of Pinot Blanc but if a wine is made from Pinot blanc grapes it should naturally be labeled as Pinot Blanc (see above).

Actually the term won wide acceptance at one time, and still unfortunately does, for a wine, good enough in its own right, made from the Chenin blanc grape (see below).

CHENIN BLANC (She-nin Blon)

A wine made from the Chenin blanc or Pineau de la Loire grape famous in France for the white wines of Anjou and Touraine of which the delightful Vouvray is the best known.

In California the Chenin blanc grape has done very well also, notably in Napa County, where it produces a very pleasing light and fruity wine, that varies from dry to quite sweet.

The modern tendency is to bottle the wine under its rightful name, Chenin Blanc. Occasionally it is still marketed as White Pinot (see above).

FOLLE BLANCHE (Fol Blonsh)

The grape is one of the principal varieties grown in the Charente district in France for the distillation of cognac. Transplanted to California it has become a much better drinking wine than in its native soil.

The wine has a rather high acid content making it useful for the production of champagne and the better grades of California chablis. It is occasionally met with as a varietal type, notably from the Napa

Valley hillsides and is tartly dry, fresh and fruity, clean both to the nose and palate. A nice, light, luncheon wine.

GREEN HUNGARIAN

The origin of the vine is obscure but is said, as the name implies, to originate in Hungry. It yields a dry wine mostly used in blending. It is, however, varietally produced, hailing from Napa, Alameda and Sonoma counties and yielding wines that are quite different in character but with their own individual charm. They are at their best when not served too cold.

WHITE RIESLING or JOHANNISBERG RIESLING
(Rees'-ling)

A premier white wine grape called Riesling in Germany where it is responsible for all the great Rhines and Moselles. It is also extensively cultivated in Alsace, Switzerland, California and elsewhere.

In California the grape is called White Riesling to distinguish it clearly from other varieties with a Riesling name such as Sylvaner or Franken Riesling, Grey Riesling and Emerald Riesling (see below under those names). Properly, the wine should be called White Riesling and is sometimes so labeled but to the confusion of retailers, restaurants and the public many growers label this wine Johannisberg Riesling naming it after some of the finest of all Riesling wines, those produced by Fürst (Prince) von Metternich at Schloss Johannisberg in the Rheingau district of Germany. This custom seems presumptuous as the correct name of White Riesling renders sufficient honor to one of California's truly great wines while trespassing on no foreign glory. Some producers market this wine with the even longer name of Johannisberger Reisling but federal regulations, thank goodness, frown on this practice and the term is bound to disappear in the near future.

White (or Johannisberg) Riesling is a most refreshing wine, with a pronounced fragrance of bouquet and a rich, satisfying flavor. Napa, Santa Clara, Santa Cruz and San Benito counties are best known for its production. Depending on the vineyard, some are lighter, delicate and pale green, others are fuller in body, fruitier and dark golden.

TRAMINER (Tra-mee'-ner) or GEWURZTRAMINER (Ge-wurts-tra-mee'-ner)

Two names for the same grape, famed in Alsace, France, and known in California as the Red Traminer on account of the red flush on its skin when ripening. The term Gewurztraminer is sometimes also used to denote selected strains of the Traminer grape.

The wines are fragrant and distinctly aromatic with a spicy scent and flavor and are generally rated as the finest rhine wine types of California after the White Rieslings. They are produced in Napa, Santa Clara and Sonoma counties.

Flora

A white, aromatic, Traminer-type variety introduced in 1958 by the University of California.

SYLVANER or Franken Riesling

The principal rhine wine type grape grown in California. It is known as the Sylvaner in Alsace, France and as the Franken Riesling in some parts of Germany. In California it is known under both names, but more correctly under that of Sylvaner.

The wines are of superior quality, fragrant and fresh with a delicate aroma and flavor. It is bottled as a varietal in Napa, Santa Clara and Sonoma counties, usually under the Sylvaner name but sometimes, presumably to take advantage of the Riesling name but leading to unnecessary confusion, as plain Riesling (see below under the white generics).

GREY RIESLING

The grape, actually the Chauché gris of France and not a Riesling at all, yields in California a soft and pleasing wine with a mild and spicy flavor. It has attained great popularity and the demand often exceeds the supply. The best known Grey Riesling comes from the Livermore Valley but it is also produced in Napa, Santa Clara and Cucamonga.

EMERALD RIESLING

A hybrid of the White Riesling and the Muscadelle, originated by the University of California at Davis.

The wine rates as a table wine of above average quality and has a clean, fresh, tart taste. The juice oxidizes and only experienced winemakers can do well with it.

Helena

Another University of California-developed grape variety. Its characteristics include a high acid content.

Veltliner (Velt′-leener)

The Red Veltliner grapes can produce an agreeable white wine, somewhat similar to Traminer (see above). The grapes have a slight pink blush when ripe which explains their name.

The wine has sufficient varietal character to warrant bottling as such. Much wine bottled as Traminer (see above) actually comes from Veltliner grapes as the two are often confused in the vineyards.

Malvasia Bianca (White Malvasia)

The grape is a muscat flavored variety of the Malvasia vines which are said to originate in Greece and are widely grown in Europe. In California it yields a sweet light table wine of delicate bouquet and flavor. It is variously labeled by its full and correct name of Malvasia Bianca and as California Malvasia without indication of color.

The wine should not be confused with the dessert wine of the same name (see page 48) nor with the scarce red Malvasia table and dessert wines.

Gold

A variety introduced primarily as a table grape, but one which produces also a light, sweet table wine with delicate muscat flavor.

B. Generics

WHITE TABLE WINE

Unassumingly named, California White Table Wine varies from average to very good indeed. It is usually dry. Many white wines, sold under fancier names, regional and other, would do as well if not better were they labeled with this simple and straightforward appellation. It is a matter of educating the public.

SAUTERNE(S), Dry, Medium and Sweet

California Sauterne is usually spelled without the final "s" of French Sauternes. A few growers use the French spelling but the general tendency is to the shorter, Americanized form.

Sauterne is produced in California from a variety of grapes, from the finest to the prolific but neutral tasting Thompson Seedless, which is actually a table grape. It ranges from dry to sweet, from straw to golden in color, while its bouquet and flavor depend on the grapes used.

Haut Sauterne has come to mean a sweet or medium sweet California Sauterne while Chateau Sauterne is reserved for the sweetest type, often made from Semillon and/or Sauvignon blanc grapes, with the addition sometimes of a little Muscadelle, the same grapes from which the best French Sauternes are also produced.

The finest California wines of the Sauternes type, outside of the Chateau wines just mentioned, are the varietal wines known as Semillon and Sauvignon Blanc (see under white varietals).

CHABLIS (Sha-blee')

The generic type of white burgundy named after the famed French wines of that name from the Chablis region.

California Chablis is pale in color, usually more delicate than sauterne, and less tart than rhine wine. It is made from a variety of grapes, from fine to indifferent.

Some excellent chablis is produced in the northern coastal counties by outstanding growers. The inexpensive ones are often not to be distinguished from dry sauterne and rhine wines of the same brand.

Rhine Wine

The California wine so labeled is made from a variety of grapes and often from the same as those from which chablis (see above) is derived but blended in such a manner that a paler, drier and tarter wine is obtained.

The best of these wines are the product of one or more of the Riesling grapes (see below) and then possess the aroma, flavor and character of the latter.

Riesling (Rees'-ling)

This wine can be a number of varietals or a blend of some or of all of them. The term has become confusing and in this writer's opinion had better be abolished altogether.

If the wine is a true varietal, made from 51% or more from either the White (Johannisberg) Riesling, the Sylvaner (Franken Riesling), the Grey Riesling or the Emerald Riesling (see under the varietal whites) it should be labeled under one of those names.

It can also be a blend of one or more of these wines without any of them predominating. The result is that California Riesling varies greatly in character and quality, depending on the grapes used, the district or vineyard of origin and the grower. It has, in fact, become a meaningless appellation.

Note: Riesling is often misspelled and mispronounced "Reisling," presumably because of an erroneous impression that it sounds more Germanic.

Moselle

This term used to be popular to designate California wine of the Rhine type. It is still occasionally used for table wines but is more familiar in describing sparkling white wines that have been carbonated.

White Chianti

This wine is marketed, like its much more popular red counterpart (see Chianti under the red generics), in raffia or straw-covered bulb-shaped bottles. Its production is very limited.

Vino Bianco

A mellow and sweetish white wine, the counterpart of Vino Rosso (see there) and labeled under different Italian names.

Light Muscat

A light wine, produced from muscat grapes, and varying from sweet to very sweet. It is sometimes labeled as California Light Sweet Wine.

Dry Muscat

A dry white wine made from muscat grapes with limited appeal.

May Wine

A white wine, flavored with waldmeister (woodruff) quite popular in Germany, especially in spring time, where it is served cold, in a bowl, with fruit in season. In California it is produced in several areas and should be better known.

Retsina

A wine of Greek origin, produced in California to a very limited extent and possessing a tang, appealing particularly to those of Greek extraction. The special flavor is due to the addition of resin (retsina).

CHART OF THE MORE PROMINENT
ROSÉ (PINK) TABLE WINES

Varietals	Generics
GRENACHE ROSÉ GAMAY ROSÉ Cabernet Rosé Zinfandel Rosé Grignolino Rosé Pinot Noir Rosé (a rarity)	Vin Rosé (Pink Wine) Rosé

IV

CALIFORNIA ROSÉ (PINK)
TABLE WINES

A. Varietals
GRENACHE ROSÉ (Gre-nash' Ro-zay)

*T*HE GRENACHE is the grape mainly responsible for the well known French rosé wines from the Tavel district in the Valley of the Rhône.

In California the Grenache is best suited to the warmest regions of the northern coastal counties where it yields one of the most typical and best rosé wines of the state. Both dry and semi-sweet types are produced in the hotter Central Valley where the variety is more at home.

GAMAY ROSÉ

Made from one of the varieties of the Gamay grape, this is an excellent wine, hailing notably from the Napa and Livermore Valleys. It is usually bottled as a varietal but is sometimes labeled simply as Rosé or Vin Rosé (see below under the Generics) or with some special proprietary name dreamed up by the grower.

Cabernet Rosé

The Cabernet Sauvignon grape yields a very good rosé table wine, bottled sometimes under the varietal name and sometimes under a proprietary label of the grower.

Zinfandel Rosé

Zinfandel is another grape that lends itself well to the production of rosés with a distinctive bouquet and flavor.

Grignolino Rosé

The Grignolino grape yields a light colored red wine in the first place and so with little effort a rosé can be produced from it. It is produced both in the Napa Valley and in the Cucamonga district.

Pinot Noir Rosé

A rare and choice rosé with distinctive character and flavor.

B. Generics

Vin Rosé (Pink Wine) or Rosé

Wines so labeled are produced from a variety of grapes including those used for the varietals (see above). Lesser grades are simply blends of red and white wines.

While the best and more typical rosé wines are dry, fruity and slightly but pleasantly tart, quite a few are on the sweeter side, containing a certain amount of residual sugar. Some are even quite sweet.

V

CALIFORNIA TABLE WINES PLUS

$\mathcal{U}$NDER REGULATIONS that went into effect July first 1959 it became permissible to market table wines containing up to 5 lbs per square inch pressure of carbon dioxide, defining in effect by law the point at which still wines are separated from sparkling wines. Actually wines containing not more than 5 lbs carbon dioxide are not effervescent. It simply allows growers to produce wines under a blanket of carbon dioxide at lower temperatures thereby obtaining more fresh, fruity flavored wines.

"Legally they can not be differentiated from their counterparts which do not contain carbon dioxide" the magazine *Wines and Vines* said; "the label can not state or even intimate that there is some carbon dioxide in the wine; nor can the wine be advertised as containing this gas. Furthermore the brand name is not supposed to give any clue to the fact that the wine has some carbon dioxide . . ."

A good many of these wines have been marketed by companies such as Gallo, United Vintners and Guild, and one or more brands of each of the three firms contains appreciable Vitis labrusca (Concord) to give an "American" or "foxy" flavor. In this, the winemakers probably took their cue from the new rage for Cold Duck sparkling wine.

CHART OF THE MORE PROMINENT
CALIFORNIA SPARKLING WINES

Varietals	Sparkling Wine Type	
Pinot Noir Chardonnay	Champagne *Nature* *Brut* *Extra Dry* *Sec* or *Dry* *Demi Sec* *Doux* or *Sweet*	really dry fairly dry medium dry to rather sweet really sweet
	Pink Champagne or Champagne Rosé	medium dry to sweet
	Red Champagne and Sparkling Burgundy	on the dry side on the sweet side
	Sparkling Muscat or Moscato Spumante Moscato Amabile	definitely sweet
	Cold Duck	sweet

VI

CALIFORNIA SPARKLING WINES

*T*HE BEST California champagnes and other sparkling wines are produced according to the French champagne method whereby the secondary fermentation which causes the sparkle takes place in the very bottle containing the wine eventually sold to the consumer. They include California champagne from very dry to sweet, California pink or Rosé Champagne and California Red Champagne.

The same wines are produced by the faster and less costly method whereby the secondary fermentation occurs in glass lined tanks or vats according to the so-called bulk or Charmat process. The law requires that sparkling wines produced in this manner be designated as "bulk process" on the label.

In both methods discussed above the wines have been fermented naturally to obtain their sparkle. So when the term "naturally fermented" appears on the labeling this only means that their sparkle has not been obtained by artificial means. Wines where the sparkle has been induced by artificial means are known as carbonated or effervescent wines and cannot be labeled as "Sparkling."

A new technique for carbonating wine invented by F. Justin Miller of Rutherford in Napa County has sparked a great deal of interest. Its main advantage lies in the fact that most artificially charged wines tend to lose their sparkle rapidly, while "Millerway" wines

retain theirs even longer than those produced by natural fermentation.

All sparkling wines are expensive due to the high federal tax
which is twenty times that on table or still wines, taxing in effect, not
so much the wine as the bubbles.

Champagne

The finest California bottle fermented champagnes and other
sparkling wines come from the northern coastal counties. Fair ones
are produced in Southern California's Cucamonga district. Bulk fermented champagnes of quality are made in these districts as well as
in the Great Inland Valley Region.

Pinot noir and Chardonnay, the grapes used to make the great
French champagnes, yield the finest California champagnes but
other grapes do very well also, such as Semillon, White Riesling,
Sylvaner, Folle blanche, and Chenin blanc.

Some, if little, varietal champagne is marketed, indicating on the
labeling that it was made from either Pinot noir or Chardonnay
grapes.

In California, as elsewhere, a so-called *dosage* or liqueuring is
added to the finished wine before inserting the final cork. This *dosage* consists of brandy, wine and sugar, the amount depending on
the degree of dryness or sweetness the producer desires to give to his
product.

Now it is a peculiar fact that people often like to fool themselves
and so it is with champagne. They like to *think* they like a dry champagne but actually they prefer it to be not so dry. That explains why
a champagne labeled *Brut* which is, or was, supposed to be very dry
indeed, may not be so very dry at all. An *Extra Dry* champagne is a
contradiction, in itself, for it is often not "dry" at all while champagnes labeled "Sec" or "Dry" are usually on the sweet side! This
system works out to satisfaction of both producer and consumer.

The driest type of champagne made, and only to a very small extent in California, is *Nature,* with no dosage added at all. This type

is really dry, though if properly made, not harsh or acid, just right. It is also the most difficult to produce.

Brut champagne is the next driest and very popular with "gourmets" and "connoisseurs" who will order no other unless it were the *Nature*. *Extra Dry* is a happy medium that will satisfy most champagne lovers while *Sec* or *Dry*, *Demi Sec* and *Doux* or *Sweet* lean progressively more to the sweet side and are dessert wines.

The dosage used in the various types will differ slightly according to the producer. Some do not indicate at all on the label what degree of dryness or sweetness their wine possesses. In such cases it is safe to assume that the champagne is in the medium range.

Pink Champagne or Champagne Rosé

A pink sparkling wine, either bottle fermented or produced in bulk fermentation. It is pretty to look at and favored by the ladies. The designation "Oeil de Perdrix" or "Partridge Eye" has sometimes been accorded this wine in California. In France the term refers to the pink tinge champagne sometimes acquires when made exclusively from dark grapes. California champagne made from Pinot noir grapes only will often have this pink hue.

Red Champagne or Champagne Rouge

A name dreamed up by growers who felt that a high quality *bottle fermented* sparkling wine should have a name other than "Sparkling Burgundy" (see below) as the latter is not required by law to indicate on the label whether it is bottle or bulk fermented.

Sparkling Burgundy

Very popular and very pretty. It is produced from a variety of grapes, is rarely bottle fermented and always on the sweet side.

Sparkling Muscat or Moscato Spumante

A sweet sparkling wine with a distinctive muscat aroma and flavor, usually produced from the Muscat of Alexandria grape.

For the Italian trade this wine is often marketed as Moscato Spumante or Gran Spumante, names reminiscent of Italy's best known sparkling wine, Asti Spumante.

Moscato Amabile

An effervescent wine, light in alcohol and very delicate, produced in the Napa Valley. The Italian word *amabile* is used to indicate, as in Italy, that the wine is sweet.

Moscato Amabile, owing to its low degree of alcohol, does not "travel well," losing its sparkle easily. It should be kept in the refrigerator and consumed soon after purchase.

Sparkling Malvasia

Made from the Malvasia bianca grape this wine has a delicate muscat character and is on the sweet side.

Cold Duck

We are at a loss to explain fully the popularity of this concoction, but then we didn't understand why Americans began drinking straight gin instead of martinis either.

Cold Duck apparently takes its name from *Kalte Ente,* a German punch made by mixing red or white table wine with *Sekt,* the German version of Champagne. Other ingredients such as lemon, sugar and brandy helped disguise the bad wines of poor vintage years.

The American Cold Duck originally came from Michigan and had a heavy flavor of Concord grapes. As the fad for so-called "pop wines" swept the country, Cold Duck began to appear in California, some containing Concord, some simple combinations of red and white sparkling wines.

Cold Duck is generally sweet and should be well chilled.

CHART OF THE MORE PROMINENT CALIFORNIA APERITIF AND DESSERT WINES

Varietals	Generics

Palomino	Sherry (*flor* and regular):
	     Pale Dry and Cocktail (dry)
	     Golden (medium)
	     Cream (sweet)

Tinta Madeira	Port Ruby Port Tawny Port Vintage Port
Muscat Frontignan Aleatico **Muscat Hamburg**	Muscatel (mostly from Muscat of Alexandria) Black Muscat
	Dry Vermouth Light Dry Vermouth Sweet Vermouth
	Marsala Madeira

VII

CALIFORNIA APERITIF
AND DESSERT WINES

*T*HESE WINES constitute about 35% of California's wine production. They are sometimes called "dessert wines" and although most of them have a relatively high sugar content there are "dry" types among them as well as all the variations between "dry" and "sweet." In this *Guide* they are grouped together as "Aperitif and Dessert Wines" for the simple reason that even the sweet types are often used as aperitifs before the meal. In fact, in the United States, the term "dessert wine" is really a complete misnomer as very few people actually serve the sweet types with the dessert. They are used between meals, as an evening refreshment or in the afternoon or morning with or without cookies or cake. Or, as stated above, as aperitif wines before the meal. It is nonsense, in this writer's opinion, to ban a sweet sherry or port, or even a muscat, before the meal as an aperitif. Many women, and even men will enjoy such a wine before the meal. Such has been, and still is the custom in many lands of the world. It is only a British custom that Port is traditionally *never* served before the dessert.

Aperitif and dessert wines used to contain about 20% alcohol per volume as against table wines which average about 12%. A new law allows 18% dessert wines and 17% Sherries. Most major wineries are shifting to the lower strengths. The higher alcoholic content is obtained by adding brandy during the fermentation of the wine. The earlier it is added, the sweeter the resulting wine will be.

The appellation of origin and the varietal designation are not nearly as usual with the California aperitif and dessert wines, as with the table wine types. With the exception, in some brands, of the Palomino grape in sherry, of the Tinta varieties in port, of Muscat Frontignan and of a few other minor instances, mention of varietal designation is absent. Most of them are also simply labeled as "California" without further indication of origin. This is a pity for just as the northern coastal counties produce the finest table wines, it is the Great Inland Valley Region that is best suited, on account of its warm to hot climate, for the production of aperitif and dessert wines. It is to be hoped that one day the fact that a Sherry or Port from either the Lodi or Fresno district, for instance, will mean as much to the public as a fine varietal table wine hailing from one of the outstanding northern coastal counties.

A. *CALIFORNIA SHERRY*

The main characteristic of sherry, wherever it is produced, is its more or less pronounced *nutty* flavor, and it is to this end that the grower develops his basic wine. Most suitable for its production in California, as in its native Spain, is the Palomino grape, also known in some wine growing districts of California as the Golden Chasselas and it is from this grape that all the finer California sherries are derived. The fact is then often indicated on the label.

California sherries are produced by two entirely different methods. Most of them are treated by the so-called heating or "baking" method, similar to that used for Madeira wines in the island of that name off the coast of West Africa. California *flor* sherries owe their special character to a process resembling that used in Spain for Spanish sherries of the drier types.

In the heating method the basic wine is fermented to the desired degree of dryness, brandy being added to check the fermentation. It is then heated in oak, redwood, concrete or steel containers for a number of weeks or months up to a year at a temperature of about 120 degrees Fahrenheit. This takes place in heated cellars or by the vats being heated by coils and at times by the warmth of the sun. When the process is completed the wine is gradually cooled and aged for the desired period of time. The oxidation taking place during the heating of the wine gives it the typical character associated with sherry.

In the *flor* process the wines usually undergo primary fermentation by a standard wine yeast to dryness. They are then fortified to ca. 15% alcohol and the growing cells of *Saccharomyces beticus* are placed on the wine's surface. This yeast, covering the wine with a flowerlike crust (hence the term *flor*), lives on the alcohol and other wine constituents and imparts to the wine, by some mysterious alchemy of nature, the characteristic flavor and tang of sherry. The wine, when fully impregnated, is brought up to full alcoholic strength and then blended and aged by the so-called "Solera" system.

This true *flor* process has been largely replaced in recent years by the "submerged *flor*" method developed at the University of California at Davis, in which yeast cells are conditioned to grow aerobically in deep tank cultures with agitation. The process is not unlike that used to produce antibiotics.

California wineries have adopted their own Solera systems which vary considerably, resembling to a greater or lesser degree the method by which sherries are aged and blended in Spain. Basically a Solera consists of an arrangement of communicating barrels or vats lying in superimposed rows, four to five tiers high. At periodic intervals the matured sherry is drawn from the bottom row to be bottled, this row being replenished from the row above and so on to the top range which is filled with new wine. In this manner the young wine mixes and ages with the older in one perpetual blend while the Solera itself was started with aged wine in the first place.

Pale or Cocktail Sherry

The drier sherries, varying from very pale and very dry to amber and dry. Some producers bottle both a Pale Dry *and* a Cocktail Sherry, the former being usually the paler and the drier of the two.

Sherry or Golden Sherry

The medium dry to medium sweet types, golden amber in color. California Sherry, without further indication, falls in this class, as does Amber Sherry.

Sweet Sherry or Cream Sherry

The sweet types, usually of a dark amber color.

Marsala

California *Marsala* is the result of a sherry blend trying to approach the character of the well-known Marsala wines from Sicily, so popular also in cooking. Herb flavored California Marsalas have also been produced.

Madeira

A few firms, following the lead of Paul Masson, now market California Madeira, similar to medium or sweet sherry.

B. *CALIFORNIA PORT*

Port has been made in California at least since the days of the Gold Rush and is one of the most popular of the so-called "dessert wines." It is often used as an aperitif as well as between meals or after dinner. Conforming to the American taste California port is, on the whole, sweeter than the port wines from Portugal. There is also, oddly enough, hardly any California *dry* port produced.

California port is produced from many different grapes, only a few of which are used for the wine in its native Portugal. To this selected group belong the popular Tinta Madeira, which yields an excellent varietal wine, Tinta Cão (sometimes blended with the former to yield Tinta port), Alvarelhão, Souzão and Touriga. Another is the Trousseau which has been identified as the Portuguese Bastardo.

California ports are generally sweet, rich, heavy bodied and fruity but often rather bland and neutral in flavor unless produced from the finer and more flavorful grapes. Young port wine, like young sherry, is apt to be "hot" to the taste buds. Older ports, and those where the better brandy has been used in their production, are naturally smoother and mellower. Some will throw a deposit and should be decanted.

Tinta Madeira

A varietal port wine made from the grape of that name and outstanding in character and flavor and fruitiness.

Tinta Port

Produced from one or more of the grapes bearing a Tinta (meaning red) name, such as Tinta Madeira, Tinta Cão. Another very fine wine.

Vintage Port

Derived from grapes harvested in a particular year. Vintage ports are usually fortified with low proof pot still brandy and bottled after one to two years wood age, so that crust may develop in the bottle. Vintage ports should be decanted.

Port and Ruby Port

Most wines labeled simply as port are ruby red and could equally well have been marketed as Ruby Port. There is often little difference, if any, between the two types when produced by the same grower.

Tawny Port

This can be a port that has been aged for considerable time in the wood, the original ruby red color turning to a russet or tawny shade.

It can also be a port made from grapes like the Trousseau which naturally yields a wine of a tawny hue.

In the cheaper brands there is often little or no difference between the tawny and other red port types, and the tawny color is the result of "baking" similar to sherry.

White Port

Nothing to do with port at all, this sweet wine is very light in color and neutral in flavor with little, if anything, to recommend it. Sometimes a decolorization process is applied to ensure its light color.

C. *CALIFORNIA MUSCATEL and MUSCAT*

These are among the sweetest of all wines and are of very ancient origin, being mentioned in literature more than 2000 years ago. The great center of California's muscat cultivation lies in the San Joaquin Valley where the grapes attain their maximum sugar content.

Muscat Frontignan

The finest California varietal muscat, delicate, golden and very sweet with a strong muscat perfume and flavor. The name is derived from the French town of Frontignan well known for its muscat wines. The grape is called Muscat Canelli from its original home of Canelli near Asti in Piedmont, Italy, where it is famed for Italian muscat wines, both still and sparkling.

Malvasia Bianca (White Malvasia)

Made from the muscat flavored grape of the same name this varietal wine, containing 20% alcohol, should not be confused with the white table wine of the same name (see there).

There is also a red Malvasia wine, produced in Southern California.

Aleatico

A soft, fruity, aromatic sweet varietal wine, sometimes called Red Muscatel. Some is produced in Southern California. At one time the grape was used to make a table wine of the same name.

Black Muscat

This is a name given to high quality red muscatels produced from Muscat Hamburg grapes or from a blend of these and Aleatico. It is one of California's foremost wines of the "dessert" type and to be recommended also as an appetizer when used with a slice of lemon.

Muscatel

Generally made from the Muscat of Alexandria grape which does so well in the San Joaquin Valley and in the Escondido district in San Diego County.

The wine varies from light to dark amber and from sweet to very sweet. It has a pronounced muscat aroma and flavor if properly made from Muscat of Alexandria grapes for considerably more than the minimum legal percentage of 51%. It is then actually a varietal although this is rarely indicated on the label.

D. *ANGELICA*

Said to have been named after the city of Los Angeles, this is one of the sweetest of all wines. Since California's early days it has been traditionally associated with the Mission grape from which much of the wine is still made. The excessive sweetness is obtained by arresting fermentation at an early stage so the must retains much of its sugar content. Amber in color, it is smooth and liqueurlike without varietal character.

E. *CALIFORNIA TOKAY*

A hybrid wine of little charm unrelated in any way to the renowned Tokay wines of Hungary.

California Tokay, amber pink in color, is a blend of angelica or other neutral wine, sherry to give a slight nutty taste, and port to lend it color. Occasionally the Flame Tokay grape, which makes such a brilliant display of its foliage in the autumn around Lodi, is used in the wine's production.

F. *CALIFORNIA VERMOUTH*

Vermouth is named after its most typical flavoring ingredient, wormwood, derived from the woody herb of that name, called *Wermuth* in German. A white wine is used as base while much of the flavoring material is imported. The wine is brought to the desired alcoholic strength and either infused and later filtered or an extract is simply added to it. Besides wormwood a host of other flavorings are used, exactly which depending on the producer and the brand.

There are two main kinds of California Vermouth, the sweet and the dry but the very light and very dry type has won separate recognition. No white *sweet* vermouth is produced, which seems a pity.

Dry Vermouth

This type is also known as French Vermouth as the wine originated and became famous in France. California Dry Vermouth is pale golden or light amber in color and averages about 18% alcohol by volume. It is made with a neutral white wine base of relatively high acid content which is fortified and blended and to which about half an ounce of herb mixture or extract is added per gallon of wine to obtain the desired character.

Light Dry Vermouth (Extra Dry,
Very Dry, Triple Dry, Dry White)

A very light and very dry vermouth created to satisfy (it is hoped)
advocates of the driest and palest of dry martinis.*

Sweet Vermouth

Also known as Italian Vermouth as it originated in that country.
It is reddish amber to brown in color, aromatic, quite sweet and contains about 16% alcohol by volume.

White wine, traditionally with some muscat, is used as a base to
which one to one and a half ounces of herbs are added per gallon
to give the wine its desired character. It is then aged in wooden
casks but for only a short period of time to prevent loss of aroma
through volatilization.

---

* Happily the craze for ever drier and ever paler martinis seems on the wane
so that the danger of a vermouthless martini looms less large than it did some
years ago. How straight or nearly straight gin can taste good to anyone remains a mystery to this writer. Three to four parts of gin to one of dry vermouth seems just about right, depending on the brands used. For the smoothest martinis try mixing them a few hours before, adding a strip of lemon peel
and storing them in the freezer.

In response to an earlier edition advocating storage of martinis overnight
in the refrigerator, Professor James F. Guymon of the University of California
wrote: "I personally disagree with mixing martinis ahead of time. Refrigerator temperature is never as low (i.e. not cold enough) as the alcohol-melting
ice mixture which can be less than o degrees C. or 32 degrees F."

VIII

CALIFORNIA FLAVORED WINES

*S*o-called "flavored wines" have made their appearance on the American market in large numbers in the relatively recent past and warrant special notice.

These wines carry proprietary names and generally have a citrus or herb flavoring. They are usually sweet (10 to 14% sugar content) and generally have the same alcoholic content (20%) as the regular types of aperitif and dessert wines.

A flavored wine may be designated legally as an aperitif wine if it contains herbs in a sufficient degree to be detected by a tasting test. Wines that do not contain herbs or that contain herbs in such minute amounts that they are not detectable in such a test may not legally be designated as aperitifs. Hence the term "flavored wines."

Exactly which flavors and herbs are used depends on the individual wine and its producer. Predominant use is made of natural citric flavors, primarily lemon and lime, and of fruit flavors such as blackberry, cherry, loganberry and raspberry. The use of rose, violet, pure vanilla and herb extractions is also indicated.

These wines are sometimes called "natural flavored wines" as the flavoring used in them is natural and not artificial or chemical.

IX

CALIFORNIA FRUIT WINES

A. *BERRY WINES*

$\mathcal{F}$RUIT WINES are produced by fermentation of fruits other than grapes, ameliorized with sugar. Most of them average around 12% alcohol by volume but a few types are also marketed at 20%, the latter being produced by the addition of spirits or of brandy from the same kind of fruit from which the wine was made.

Berry Wines

California has the largest berry production of any state in the union. All berry wines are fruity and sweet, each with the typical character and more or less pronounced flavor of the particular berry from which it is derived.

Blackberry Wines

The blackberry or bramble is a native of temperate regions and is particularly abundant on the Pacific Coast. There are over 600 named varieties of the blackberry of which the boysenberry (see below) is the best known for wine production in California.

Blackberry wine is produced at both 12% and 20% alcohol by volume.

Blackberry Wine of the Boysenberry Variety

Boysenberries constitute by far the greater part of the blackberries grown in the United States. They are black when ripe with a slight blue or purple tinge. The wine they yield has an especially distinctive aroma and flavor. It is produced both at 12% and at 20% alcohol by volume.

Elderberry Wine

This wine is made from the umbrella shaped berry clusters of the American or sweet elder. It is purplish red and has the typical tangy flavor of the fruit. 12% alcohol by volume.

Loganberry Wine

The berry was named after Judge J. H. Logan who raised it from seed in his garden at Santa Cruz, California, in 1881. The wine is brilliant red and has a pronounced fruity flavor. 12% alcohol by volume.

Raspberry Wine

Made from the red raspberry and having the delicate aroma and flavor of that fruit. 12% alcohol by volume.

Red Currant Wine

Produced from the small tangy berries of the red currant shrub from which the popular jelly is also made. The wine is light red, less sweet than other berry wines and contains 12% alcohol by volume.

Strawberry Wine

California's Santa Clara Valley is famed for its strawberries. Much of the strawberry wine is also produced there. It is delicate in flavor and has an alcoholic content of 12% by volume.

B. *FRUIT WINES OTHER THAN BERRY WINES*

Apple Wine

California apple wine is made princpially from Gravenstein apples which are specially well suited for the purpose because of their flavor, high sugar content and juiciness. They are grown mainly in the vicinity of Santa Rosa and Sebastopol in Sonoma County. The wine is usually bottled at 20% alcohol by volume.

Apricot Wine

Although this beverage is not produced in large quantities in California, it, as is cherry wine, is popular with Scandinavian-Americans. The alcohol content usually is about 12% by volume.

Cherry Wine

The best cherry wine is made from the sour or pie type cherry which gives the wine a brilliant red color and a pronounced fruity flavor. 12% alcohol by volume.

Peach Wine

A less familiar fruit wine, containing 12% or 20% alcohol by volume.

Pear Wine also called **Perry**

Occasionally met with and containing 12% alcohol by volume.

Part Two

X

NOTABLE WINERIES BY
REGION AND DISTRICT

*T*HERE ARE two accepted ways of classifying the wine growing districts of California.

The first, as worked out by the viticultural scientists of the University of California, is of primary interest to the growers. The method
is based on the adaptability of the different grape varieties to the
climatic conditions of the various wine growing localities of the
state. These have been grouped, regardless of location, according to
the average degrees of heat above 50° Fahrenheit from April 1 to
October 31, and correspond to what can be termed the cool, moderately cool, intermediate, moderately hot and hot climatic zones.

The type of soil, naturally, also influences the grape as to the character of the wine it will yield. Even so, the vine draws much of its
nourishment from the surrounding atmosphere, the leaves of all
plants nourishing themselves by breathing in the air.

The second system is the geographical one, which makes it possible to progress from region to region and from district to district or
county. This makes it easy to follow the various wine growing districts on a map and is the method utilized by this *Guide.*

The geographical system is also preferable for the purpose of this

Guide, as many wineries obtain grapes, and sometimes wines, from vineyards located in more than one climatic zone, be it from their own vines or from other growers, and either from the same general area or from other districts. Growers in the inland valley often produce table wines from grapes grown in the coastal districts, or blend them with the valley wines, and coastal growers often make aperitif and dessert types from grapes grown in the inland valley areas.

Whether or not a wine has been wholly produced by the grower is indicated on the labeling. The term "produced and bottled" means that a minimum of 75% of the wine has been produced, that is, fermented into wine, by the grower whose name appears on the label. "Made and bottled" means that at least 10% of the wine has actually been produced and that the balance has received some cellar treatment by the grower on the label, although it may not have been produced in his winery. The difference between the two methods of production does not necessarily indicate a graduation in quality among wines, although wineries are naturally the proudest of those wines which they themselves have wholly grown and produced. Wineries which only market the latter are sometimes described as having a chateau operation. Such wines are, or can be designated as "estate bottled."

The more notable wineries of California are presented in the following pages by region and district. In each district they are arranged alphabetically within the locality. Selection has been governed by the quality, both of premium and standard quality wines produced. No prices are indicated, as they will vary according to the part of the country where they are purchased.

A complete listing of all California wineries is published in the "Annual Directory Issue" of the publication *Wines and Vines,** while a practical series of Guide Maps, arranged by county, is available at the Wine Institute.†

* 703 Market Street, San Francisco 94103.
† 717 Market Street, San Francisco 94103.

The California wine producing areas can be grouped geographically in three great regions, as follows:

The cool to moderately cool *northern coastal region,* where all the finest table wines are produced, the top quality champagnes, and some notable aperitif and dessert wines.

The hot *inland valley region,* the home especially of the aperitif and dessert wines, but producing also table wines and bulk fermented champagnes.

The warm *Southern California region,* where aperitif and dessert wines, champagnes, and table wines of note are produced.

XI

THE NORTHERN COASTAL REGION

$\mathcal{T}$HIS REGION, sometimes referred to as that of the northern coastal counties, lies close to the coast north and south of San Francisco and takes in the wine growing districts west of the coastal range of mountains. They are, from north to south:

The *Sonoma-Mendocino, Napa Valley-Solano, Alameda-Contra Costa* and the *Santa Clara-Santa Cruz-San Benito* districts, lying respectively northwest, northeast, southeast and south of the Golden Gate.

A. *SONOMA-MENDOCINO DISTRICT*

This district consists of the two counties which have given it their joint names. Sonoma County yields some premium table wines and champagnes which rate among the finest of the state. It also produces vast quantities of standard quality table wine, mostly red.

Sonoma, with nearly thirty bonded wineries and wine cellars, ranks third behind Napa and Santa Clara among all California counties in number of winemaking plants. Its wines can conveniently be grouped according to the three valleys where they are produced: the Sonoma, Santa Rosa and Russian River valleys.

SONOMA COUNTY—SONOMA VALLEY

The appellation Sonoma Valley is restricted in the *Guide* to denote the valley proper. The name has often been loosely applied to a larger area, taking in the neighboring Santa Rosa Valley, but the latter is actually part of the Russian River basin and is therefore treated separately. Sonoma Valley is some eleven miles long and is named after Sonoma Creek, which empties in San Pablo Bay to the south.

Sonoma Valley is familiar to many as the Valley of the Moon, made famous in literature by Jack London, who wrote and died there, not far from the ruins of the once famous Kohler winery, destroyed by the great earthquake of 1906.

The Valley of the Moon, or of the Moons, as the Indians used to call it, does its name full justice, for, separated from the Napa Valley to the east by the Mayacamas Range, the moon, to those down below, seems to rise, not once, but many times among the succeeding mountain peaks.

Oddly enough, though the region is known far beyond the borders of California, only one winery, the Valley of the Moon Winery founded in 1944 at Glen Ellen, takes its name from the area.

Buena Vista Winery Inc., Sonoma

It seems only suitable to begin the presentation of the wineries of California with Buena Vista, once the home of Haraszthy, the "father of modern California viticulture."

Agoston Haraszthy, a man of temperament and of many talents, came from a noble Hungarian family. Because of wanderlust or because he aided in plotting Magyar independence, he left his Hungarian domain and sailed for America. He first settled in Wisconsin, where he founded the town of Haraszthy, which was to become Sauk City. Known as the "Count," he later shed this title for the more democratic one of "Colonel."

In 1849 he came West, to San Diego, which he helped to develop and where he was elected the town's first sheriff. He later represented that county as state assemblyman and moved north to Sacramento. San Francisco, thriving with the Gold Rush, next attracted the colonel's energetic spirit and he became the official melter and refiner of the U.S. Mint. He landed in difficulties, accused of exceeding his legal limit of gold wastage, but was absolved by the court and his name completely cleared.

Haraszthy had been interested in viticulture ever since his early Hungarian days. In California he had planted vineyards near San Diego and in San Francisco near Mission Dolores as well as at Crystal Springs, in what is now San Mateo. He realized, from the example of Jean Louis Vignes at Los Angeles, that the better California wines were produced from European grape varieties and he himself had already imported many such vines, including, as had been widely accepted, the one he named and became known as Zinfandel.

Haraszthy finally chose Sonoma as the ideal place to realize his ambition of establishing the finest vineyards in California. He became a neighbor of the pioneer grower General Vallejo, who produced a wine of great repute, Lachryma Montis, named after his estate. The two families became friendly rivals in wine making, and became much closer than friends when the double wedding took place at the Mission San Francisco de Solano in Sonoma in 1863, uniting Natalia and Jovita, daughters of General Vallejo, to Attila and Arpad Haraszthy, sons of the colonel.

Haraszthy had named his country place Buena Vista because of the sweeping view of the Sonoma Valley and San Francisco Bay and here he constructed an imposing Pompeian mansion. Hundreds of acres of vines were planted and a series of tunnels dug deep in the hillside for cellar accommodation. Skilled viticulturists came to work at Buena Vista, among them Charles Krug, who was himself to become one of California's leading wine growers.

It was at Buena Vista that Haraszthy wrote his classic "Report on Grapes and Wines of California." He advised all growers to test as many varieties as possible, to cultivate those which throve the best and produced the finest wines. He was certain that California could yield "as noble a wine as any country on the face of the globe."

In 1861 Haraszthy was appointed by Governor John G. Downey to report on wine growing in Europe. From a viticultural point of view the trip was a great success. He visited all the important European wine growing districts and collected some 100,000 cuttings from 300 grape varieties, all of which he planted on his return. Financially the journey proved a source of discord. The California Legislature refused to pay the expenses incurred, but the colonel could find consolation in being made president of the California Agricultural Society.

Haraszthy had reached the summit of his prestige. The fame of Buena Vista wines had spread far; offices of the company were operating in San Francisco, in Chicago, New York, Philadelphia and London. In October 1864 Colonel and Mrs. Haraszthy were hosts at a Vintage Ball and Masquerade, the social event of the time.

Then financial and other troubles succeeded each other rapidly. Phylloxera struck, Haraszthy suffered losses on the Stock Exchange, taxes on spirits wiped out his profit on brandy, a fire raged at Buena Vista, ruining much of the wine, credit was cut off from the bank, and financial assistance from other sources proved unavailable.

So the "father of California's modern wine industry" left Buena Vista, Sonoma, and California for good. He went to Nicaragua, where he obtained a government contract for the distillation of spirits from sugar and there he started a new domain. But one day, in July 1869, he vanished. It is believed that he tried to cross an alligator infested stream by means of an overhanging branch which broke off by his weight and plunged him to his doom. The life of a great American pioneer had come to a tragic end.

In California Attila and Arpad Haraszthy continued the family wine making tradition. Arpad became famous for his "Eclipse" Champagne, while Attila stayed on at Buena Vista to fight the phylloxera, which was not conquered till the turn of the century. The estate suffered a further great blow when the 1906 earthquake brought down in ruins much of the winery and caved in the storage tunnels, burying, so it is believed, much champagne beneath the debris. Buena Vista entered a dormant period in wine making which lasted till 1943.

In that year Frank H. Bartholomew, now chairman emeritus of United Press International (U.P.I.), acquired a large acreage of the former Buena Vista vineyards and revived the society, restoring also the two stone wineries from Harazsthy's days.

In 1968, a $2 million corporation was formed to construct a third winery building. The winery itself was sold to Young's Markets of Los Angeles and Bartholomew retained the vineyards and ranch. Vernon O. Underwood of Los Angeles, president of Young's, joined the company as chairman of the board. Philip C. Gaspar is president.

The following premium wines are available under the *Buena Vista* label:

Table wines:

RED: Cabernet Sauvignon and Pinot Noir (Estate Bottled), Zinfandel (from the vineyards where the wine grew to fame), Burgundy, Lachryma Montis (a red dinner wine);

WHITE: Pinot Chardonnay (Estate Bottled), White Riesling Johannisberger (Estate Bottled), Gewurztraminer (Estate Bottled, Vintage), Sylvaner (Estate Bottled, Vintage), Sonoma Sauterne (Vintage), Green Hungarian (a *Buena Vista* specialty), Chablis, Vine Brook (from *Sylvaner* grapes, Vintage), Grey Riesling (Estate Bottled);

ROSÉ: Rose Brook (from Cabernet Sauvignon grapes, Estate Bottled) and Zinfandel Rosé;

Champagne (Bottle fermented): Pinot Chardonnay Champagne (Brut, Estate grown);

Sparkling: Zinfandel, Cabernet Sauvignon Rosé;

Aperitif and Dessert Wines: Ultra Dry Sherry, Golden Sherry and Cardinal Port (all finished in small oak casks).

Hacienda Wine Cellars, Sonoma

As noted above, when Frank Bartholomew sold the Buena Vista Winery, he retained the vineyards he had restored with the help of Andre Tchelistcheff (see Beaulieu Vineyard). He agreed to supply grapes to Buena Vista for a period of years while the new owners developed a vineyard of their own, about 400 acres now in production in the Carneros district on the Napa-Sonoma county line. Meanwhile, Bartholomew began work on a new winery, which he named *Hacienda Wine Cellars*.

He converted a two-story Spanish-style brick building on the ranch into a handsome winery and visitors center, with attractive wine gardens overlooking the vineyards. New equipment from Germany, France and the United States was purchased, and the first crush, of Chardonnay grapes purchased from other growers, was made in 1973. The same year Hacienda finished a cocktail sherry, and in 1974 Pinot Noir, Gewurtz Traminer and Zinfandel were added to the line. The operation is still small, but it's bound to grow.

"We sell only to visitors," Bartholomew said, "since this time I am determined to control the growth of the business against thyroid-type growth and inflation.

"We are under continuous pressure to sell to restaurants and stores, but thus far, since our limited production will hardly keep up with the demand at the front door, we have restricted ourselves, and I dare say will continue to do so for a while yet."

Nonetheless, the quality of the wines is such that distribution is likely to expand eventually, and the label probably will be seen in better wine shops before long.

The general manager is Arlie Brett, who had been with Bartholomew for 20 years; the winemaker is Steven McRostie, who has a master's degree from Davis; the vineyard and nursery foreman is Don Van Staaveren, assisted by Donald Jones, and the sales manager is John F. Schallert.

Hanzell Vineyards, Sonoma

The reason for the existence of the beautiful Hanzell Vineyards high in the hills behind Sonoma overlooking the romantic Valley of the Moon is simple but inspiring.

After returning home from Italy where he had served as Chief of the Marshall Plan from 1948 to 1950 the well known businessman, financier and diplomat J. D. Zellerbach and Mrs. Zellerbach bought a country place in the Sonoma Valley. Highly appreciative of fine wines the thought came naturally to establish vineyards on the hillsides sloping down from the house. A perfectionist and partial to the great burgundies of France, Mr. Zellerbach had his vineyards of some 16 acres planted exclusively to Pinot noir and Chardonnay, responsible for the glories of his favorite Romanée Conti and Montrachet. From that developed the idea of building a model winery and making his own wine, the finest California could produce. It was to be an operation in the grand manner and great traditions. Experts, including sages of the University of California, were consulted in the layout of the vineyards and in equipping the winery, inspired by Burgundy's Clos de Vougeot. No effort was spared in securing the best of everything. Winery equipment was specially designed at great expense, glass lined stainless steel tanks of the most modern type were installed, small Limousin oak cooperage was imported from Nuits St. Georges in Burgundy and an up to date and efficient laboratory was provided. The winery was named Hanzell Vineyards, a contraction of Hana, as Mrs. Zellerbach is called, and of the family name.

When Ambassador Zellerbach died just before the 1963 harvest, many connoisseurs wondered out loud what would happen to his "great experiment." They were relieved when Hanzell wines, made with exactly the same care and devotion as before, returned to the market under the aegis of the late Douglas N. Day, a retired supermarket chain executive who purchased the Zellerbach Sonoma estate in 1965. His first crush took place that fall, and the wines, still Pinot Noir and Chardonnay exclusively, were bottled in 1967. Mr. Day died in 1970, but the winery continued under family ownership.

The new owners altered little at Hanzell. Bradford Webb, the winery's original chemist and *maître de chai,* was retained as chief consultant. The winemaker now is Kim Giles. New Limousin oak barrels from France replaced those casks removed from the winery when the previous vintages were sold by the Zellerbach estate.

To the Days, operating the winery was not a business, "it's more like raising a child."

"The objective that motivated the development of Hanzell continues to prevail today," Mr. Day said. "Many knowledgeable enophiles consider that the two wines of Hanzell are the two finest of their types produced in California. Certainly the current demand for the wines is sufficient tribute. We have been forced to accept orders on a reservation basis only."

After her husband's death, Mrs. Day added another storage room for Pinot Noir and cleared four more acres to plant Chardonnay vines grafted from the same stocks in the original vineyards. Even so, she said, "the demand for our Chardonnay is far greater than we can supply."

Sebastiani Vineyards, Sonoma

This winery, one of the largest producers in Sonoma County and the oldest wine enterprise in the Sonoma Valley operated continuously by one family, was founded in 1904 by Samuele Sebastiani who immigrated from Italy at an early age. From a small beginning—the 501 gallon tank he purchased from the old Bullotti Winery—he gradually built up his enterprise through hard work, a strong determination to succeed and a deep faith in spiritual assistance.

During the 40 years that Samuele Sebastiani was a prominent figure in the Sonoma wine industry his operation grew to be Northern California's largest individually owned winery with a cooperage of one and three quarters million gallons. He shared his success with many about him, building homes for his workers and donating a parochial school. For the people of Sonoma he built streets for the town, an apartment house, a theatre, an auto court, recreational facilities and completed many other projects.

When Samuele Sebastiani retired his son August took over, putting much energy into wine making, distillation processes and improvements in general. His father, however, never failed to visit the winery until his death in 1944.

Some vineyards are owned in the Sonoma Valley but most of the wines are produced from grapes purchased year after year from the same growers. The winery's operation was mostly on a bulk wine basis supplying other wineries and bottlers throughout the nation when August Sebastiani decided in 1954 to begin bottling his own wines. Much money went into research while the know-how and experience were already present. To get the full flavor of the Sebastiani enterprise let us quote August Sebastiani owner and general manager:

"We inherit that peculiarly favorable grape soil of Sonoma, a bountiful sky of rain and sunshine, and a people willing to work and to take great pride in their product. We are proud of what we produce."

There is no doubt that August Sebastiani is a man who inherits the love of wine making from his father and who possesses the industrial skill of an organizer with modern ideas based on old but dynamic and proved methods. A charming host and a dedicated person he lives with his closely knit family on a hilltop right in Sonoma not far from his beloved winery. Many medals in the winery's sampling room testify to the family ability in wine making.

Sebastiani Vineyards produces tables wines, aperitif and dessert wines, including vermouths. August Sebastiani is particularly proud of his Tuscan wine making methods. The rewards are obvious in his Barbera, a hearty, ruby red varietal. He and his able and energetic son, Sam, also have a right to be pleased with the public response to their Green Hungarian, Gamay Beaujolais and Zinfandel.

In the summer of 1971 the Sebastianis completed a sun-heated aging area for Solera sherries and ports, and in 1974 they finished construction of a unique fermentation cellar containing 56 individually temperature-controlled stainless steel tanks of six different sizes. "We don't intend to get bigger," August Sebastiani said, "but we never stand still in our attempt to get better."

ZD Wines, Sonoma

The name of this new operation in the tiny hamlet of Vineburg hard by Sonoma comes from the last initials of the partners who own it, Gino Zepponi and Norman deLeuze. Aerospace and optics engineers respectively, they established the winery in 1969 as a hobby and retirement plan. Their first wines, Pinot Noir and White Riesling, were produced that year, and a Gewurztraminer was added in 1970.

All ZD wines are and will be 100 per cent varietals, the partners said, and all are aged in 50-gallon oak casks in their small but efficient air-conditioned winery.

In addition to the wines already mentioned, Chardonnay and a small amount of Flora are produced, all from grapes purchased from growers in the Carneros area in Napa County. A Zinfandel from the Shenandoah Valley, a rolling foothill region in Amador County, was added in 1973 and 1974.

Visits to the winery must be arranged by mail, the same method by which most ZD wines are sold.

Grand Cru Vineyards, Glen Ellen

This winery, which was established in 1970 and had its first crush in 1971, is located in an old stone building among vineyards that actually date back to the 1880s when the estate was set out and later planted by a Frenchman named Francis Lamoine. The winery managed to survive several fires and the 1906 earthquake, was sold to a family that produced bulk wines, was closed during Prohibition, reopened after Repeal and finally went out of business altogether in the early 1950s.

The restoration was undertaken by a group of young people headed by president, general manager and vineyard foreman Allen Ferrera, who was formerly in electronics and plant management, and winemaker Robert Magnani, a member of a winemaking family whose own background was in electronics and engineering.

Grand Cru (French for great growth) has 36 acres, including part of the original Lamoine vineyard, planted to Zinfandel and Gewurztraminer, the latter marketed for the first time in 1974. The rest of the production is limited to four Zinfandels, one of them among the few white wines of the variety made in California. It is a pale yellow table wine, difficut to achieve from the deeply colored, "bloody" Zinfandel grape. A new project is the creation of a dessert wine by artificially infecting Gewurztraminer grapes on trays with *Botrytis cinerea*, or "noble mold."

The winery is two miles north of Glen Ellen and is open to the public on weekends and holidays. Visits may be arranged by appointment during the week.

Kenwood Vineyards, Kenwood

Like Grand Cru a few miles to the south, Kenwood Vineyards is a rebirth of an old winery, but this one never fell into decay. Originally it was the Pagani Winery, founded in 1906 by Julius and John Pagani, who came from Italy and specialized in making sound, country jug wines and bulk wine for other companies. After the winery and vineyards were purchased by a group of enophiles headed by John Sheela and Martin Lee Jr. in 1970, the emphasis shifted to premium varietals, but they continued to make good, inexpensive generics.

A new French press and small, American oak barrels were added to the existing redwood tanks, and production was started on a line of quality table wines under the direction of winemaker Bob

Koslowsky. Grapes used to come not only from Kenwood-owned vineyards, but also from other areas of the North Coast.

The wines include Mountain Red, White and Rosé jug wines, generic Burgundy and Chablis, and Johannisberg Riesling, Chardonnay, Petite Sirah, Cabernet Sauvignon, Zinfandel and Barbera. All but the Barbera among the varietals are vintage dated. Kenwood Vineyards also has made Gamay, Ruby Cabernet, Grey Riesling, Green Hungarian and Chenin Blanc, and some of these wines likely will continue to be available. All are sold at the winery ten miles north of Sonoma, and limited national marketing began as production increased.

Sonoma County—Santa Rosa Valley

The Santa Rosa Creek, after which the valley is named, empties its waters eventually in the Russian River. The city of Santa Rosa is where the Luther Burbank home is to be found. The famed botanist and horticulturist, who was also greatly interested in viticulture, lies buried beneath the cedar of Lebanon in the city park.

Martini & Prati Wines, Inc., Santa Rosa

Some eight miles northwest of Santa Rosa, near Forestville, lies the extensive Martini and Prati Winery, operated by Elmo Martini* and Edward Prati.

The Martini family have been in the wine business in Santa Rosa since the eighteen seventies. Raphaele Martini bought the present winery and vineyards shortly after the turn of the century, the enterprise being expanded at various times and later operated by his sons. In 1943 the property was purchased by the Hiram Walker interests, owners of W. A. Taylor and Company, but in 1950 the winery and vineyards reverted back to Elmo Martini, in partnership with Enrico Prati of Italian Swiss Colony fame and with the latter's son Edward.

* Not to be confused with Louis Martini of St. Helena, Napa County.

Enrico Prati passed away in 1952 and Elmo Martini is now president of the company, while Edward Prati, who also owns vineyards of his own, is secretary-treasurer.

The winery is the second largest in Sonoma County. The featured brands are *Martini & Prati* and *Fountaingrove,* the latter label having been purchased from the owner of Fountaingrove Ranch, once a famed winery.

SONOMA COUNTY—RUSSIAN RIVER VALLEY

The Russian River finds its source in Mendocino County and flows south into Sonoma, turning west past Healdsburg to empty in the Pacific Ocean some ten miles beyond Guerneville.

The lower Russian River Valley, around Guerneville, forms a small, separate wine growing area, where some of the finest California champagne is produced. The inland or upper section of the valley takes in the area around Healdsburg northwards to Cloverdale and on into Mendocino County.

As in other California vineyard areas, new wineries proliferated in the 1960s and 1970s, and grape acreage was expanded most dramatically in the Alexander Valley near Geyserville, where prune orchards and other crops were ripped out to plant the expensive vineyards everyone thought would yield liquid gold.

Several new small wineries, such as Russian River Vineyards and Joseph Swan Vineyards, founded in Forestville in 1964 and 1969 respectively, Vina Vista Vineyards established at Geyserville in 1971 and Dry Creek Vineyard at Healdsburg in 1972, joined a number of older wineries that had been producing country wines for years, like Cambiaso Winery and Vineyard located at Healdsburg since 1934, and A. Rege Wine Co. and Bandiera Wines, operating in Cloverdale since 1939 and 1957.

F. Korbel & Brothers, Inc., Guerneville

The great, castle-like Korbel winery, standing among vineyards and huge tree stumps, is situated on the bank of the Russian River a few miles east of Guerneville, just beyond Rio Nido. It is the home of champagnes that rate among the finest of California and are known throughout the nation and beyond.

It was founded by the Korbels, a story of enterprise dating back to the days of the pioneers.

The Korbel brothers, Francis, Anton and Joseph, were born in the little town of Behine in Bohemia, now part of Czechoslovakia. They emigrated to the United States and came to San Francisco in the early eighteen sixties. Ironworkers and machinists by trade they soon found employment in machine shops. Francis, the eldest, built a cigar box factory, aided by his brothers, and such was the beginning of a family enterprise that led by stages to lithography, lumber, the building of a sawmill on the Russian River and finally to the production of wine and champagne.

When all the virgin timber had been cut—the vast stumps of which remain an impressive sight today—the Korbels sought the advice of the University of California on what to raise on the newly cleared land. After a dairy venture that proved unsuccessful vines were planted with the purpose of selling the grapes to Sonoma wineries. When the first crop was harvested grape prices proved to be so low that the Korbels decided to crush the grapes themselves and so they landed in the wine business.

The original winery still stands and in 1886 the first section of the present winery was constructed from lumber and brick made on the property. Table wines were produced at first but in the nineties it was decided to make champagne as well and the latter became the sole business of Korbel Brothers after the second World War.

In early 1954 the Korbel family, headed by Anton and Leo Korbel, sold the corporation to the Heck brothers, another dynasty of wine makers. Adolf L. Heck is president of the company and the champagne producer, Paul R. is executive vice president, taking care of the 2,200 acre ranch and of the initial wine production while Ben A. Heck is vice president in charge of sales.

The grandfather of the Heck brothers started the family wine business by owning and operating a small winery in Alsace-Lorraine, at that time part of Germany. His son, Adolf Heck, the father of the Heck brothers, knew about wine making from an early age, and came to this country shortly after the turn of the century, going into the wine business in Chicago. In 1933, with the advent of Repeal, the family moved to St. Louis where Adolf Heck senior took over the operation of the American Wine Company, producers at that time of Cook's Imperial Champagne. He remained president and general manager until his death in 1946. The American Wine Company having been acquired by the Schenley interests, the Heck brothers went with National Distillers, remaining in the wine business at Italian Swiss Colony. In 1954 the opportunity arose to buy the Korbel winery, something the Heck brothers had been waiting for. And so the name of Heck became identified with that of Korbel in the field of premium wine making.

Quality is the Heck brothers philosophy. They do not believe in making the public drink what they think it should have but rather in giving the public what it wants and making it as well as possible.

The most important varietal grapes raised at the ranch for the production of sparkling wines are Pinot noir, Pinot blanc, Chardonnay, French Colombard and Sauvignon blanc. Some White Riesling and Sylvaner are also grown.

Under the ownership of the Heck brothers bottle fermented Champagnes continue to be featured, made by the original French Champagne process. They are marketed under the *Korbel* brand, as follows:

Korbel Natura (very dry, made especially for gourmets), Korbel Brut (dry), Korbel Extra Dry (medium dry), Korbel Sec (medium dry), Korbel Rouge (red champagne or sparkling burgundy, on the dry side) and Korbel Rosé (a pink champagne marketed in a transparent bottle, delicately sweet).

The Heck brothers added a light brandy to their line, and now it is one of the best-selling in the nation. Later they entered the aperitif and dessert wine field, and now offer three Sherries and a Port in addition to a complete line of table wines. All are sold under the *Korbel* label, including Cabernet Sauvignon, Pinot Noir, Burgundy, Zinfandel, Chateau Vin Rosé, Chablis, Sonoma Blanc (Fumé Blanc), Gray Riesling, Pinot Chardonnay and Johannisberg Riesling, the latter two first released early in 1975.

In 1954 the Heck brothers purchased the nearby Santa Nella winery and have since remodeled to provide facilities for all of Korbel's crushing, fermenting and intermediate storage. A new bottling plant for table wines and a case goods warehouse have been added adjacent to the main winery building.

Exceptionally thorough winery tours are conducted three times a day by knowledgeable guides, ending in a cathedral-like tasting room.

Sonoma Vineyards (Tiburon Vintners), Windsor

This company was founded in 1960 by Rodney D. Strong, who remains its board chairman. In 1963 he took over a 68-year-old winery at Windsor eight miles north of Santa Rosa, and at the time of this writing, the corporation he established with Peter Friedman, now president, owns or controls Sonoma and Mendocino County vineyards totaling 5,000 acres. The vineyard manager is Richard McDowell and the production manager is William Bagge.

In 1971 the company dedicated a new $1.5 million winery complex, one of the most modern in the state. The 30,000-square-foot structure took a year to build, and is a far cry from the days when Strong bought bulk wines from other makers, bottled and labelled them under Tiburon Vintners.

The name of the company was officially changed to Sonoma Vineyards, and under that label its wines are marketed in stores in 30 states. Wines of the *Windsor Vineyards* label still are sold to direct-mail customers in case lots with specially printed labels to honor any individual or commemorate any occasion. Tasting rooms are maintained at the main office in Tiburon on the north shore of San Francisco Bay and at the winery in Windsor.

In addition to Sherry and Port, most table wines are available under the *Windsor Vineyards* label.

Sonoma Vineyards, like many other wineries in California, borrowed heavily at high interest rates to finance its expansion during the boom of the early 70s, and late in 1975 the directors agreed to a deal under which control of the firm eventually would shift to the Renfield Corp., a New York importing and distribution company.

Davis Bynum Winery, Healdsburg

When Davis Bynum finally opened his own winery in 1965, it was the culmination of a long dream. A newspaperman who spent 15 years working for the *San Francisco Chronicle*, he acquired his appreciation of fine wines from his father, University of California historian and executive Lindley Bynum, author of "California Wines and How to Enjoy Them."

Dave wanted to establish his winery in the urban area to give his clients an opportunity to see all the operations—trucking in grapes, crushing, fermenting, racking, bottling, etc.—so he located on a busy downtown street in Albany next to Berkeley. However as the reputation for Davis Bynum wines grew and the demand for national distribution began to be felt, the Albany plant became too small and inconvenient.

The expansion began when he started crushing grapes in St. Helena in 1968. In 1973 a new corporation was formed including several Russian River Valley growers whose grapes are crushed and estate-bottled by Bynum. The new winery, modern and well equipped, was converted out of an old hop kiln building, a holdover from the days before Sonoma County's hop farms succumbed to plant disease in the early fifties. The grower–shareholders have a total of about 400 acres of Russian River vineyards, the company itself owns another 26 acres in the Napa Valley and Bynum planned to plant an additional 30 acres adjacent to the winery, which is on a portion of the River Bend Ranch in the Sweetwater Springs area, about eight miles southwest of Healdsburg. Although the Albany tasting room was to be moved to a new location, it would not be at the winery, Bynum said, because "we want to devote our full attention here to the production of premium wines."

In spite of the expansion, the winery remains a family-oriented affair, with Bynum's wife, Dorothy, running the tasting room and their son, Hampton, assistant winemaker.

The brands available are *Davis Bynum Private Reserve* for limited bottlings of exceptionally fine wines, *Davis Bynum* for premium wines and *Barefoot Bynum*, the colorful label for jug wines. Several generics are sold in addition to a full line of quality varietals, and the winery offers two Ports and four Sherries, including an excellent seven-year-old Amber Dry Sherry.

L. Foppiano Wine Company, Healdsburg

The winery dates back to the early eighteen eighties and was known as the Smith winery when the late Louis Foppiano, the father and namesake of the present owner, purchased it in 1898. The company is strictly a family concern.

Louis Foppiano was born right on the property, in the building which now houses the company's offices. Raised in the business since his earliest days, he has built it into a prosperous concern, with vineyards over 200 acres.

In the early seventies the Foppianos began to market their wines nationally and started to produce varietal wines of constantly improving quality. The first were released in 1972, and Louis Foppiano was particularly happy with the 1973 Cabernet Sauvignon and Pinot Noir, two wines not previously made.

A full line of sound and reasonably-priced jug wines, including a very good Zinfandel, is available under the *Foppiano Vineyards* label. Vintage-dated varietals labeled *Foppiano Russian River Valley* include estate-bottled Petite Sirah, Gamay Beaujolais, Cabernet Sauvignon and Pinot Noir, as well as another Zinfandel.

Simi Winery, Healdsburg

From a small, regional, family-owned winery started in 1876, Simi evolved rapidly in the 1970s to become part of an international beverage combine, Scottish & Newcastle Importers Co., the American subsidiary of a big British brewing and distilling firm. Nevertheless the head winemaker, Mary Ann Graf, a gamin-like 1965 Davis graduate who joined Simi in 1972, sees a future of controlled growth and finer wines. "No one at Simi wants to stand pat," she said, "but neither do any of us want to see Simi grow so quickly to a point that the character of the winery is lost in the process, something all of us have seen happen in other instances."

Under the ownership of the Simi family, the winery achieved a wide reputation for good wines, especially in the period following Prohibition. By the 1960s activity had slowed down, and in 1970 Mrs. Isabella Simi Haigh, daughter of one of the founders, sold out to Russell Green, former president of the Signal Oil & Gas Co., who had been growing grapes for several years at his summer place in the adjacent Alexander Valley. He hired Andre Tchelistcheff, dean of American winemakers, as a consultant, and Mary Ann Graf became winemaker. Both stayed on after Scottish & Newcastle bought the operation from Green in 1974. Fred E. Aurelio has been named president.

In addition to a large quantity of aging red wines, some dating back to Repeal, Green acquired an old stone winery in need of repair and expansion. An attractive tasting room and a cool picnic garden were built, new fermenting equipment and small cooperage were installed and a modern laboratory was developed. "Part of the winemaker's art is to combine, judiciously, modern technology and traditional techniques," winemaker Graf said. "Otherwise, what do they hire us for?"

In addition to a generic Burgundy, premium varietals include Chardonnay, Johannisberg Riesling, Gewurztraminer, Cabernet Sauvignon, Pinot Noir and Carignane, seldom seen bottled under its own name. A dry Rosé of Cabernet Sauvignon rounds out the list.

Geyser Peak Winery, Geyserville

Another winery founded in the nineteenth century and recently purchased by a national corporation (in this case the Schlitz Brewing Co.), Geyser Peak was unusual in that it had not been selling wines under its own name. The Bagnani family, which acquired it in 1937, produced bulk wines and wine vinegar.

In 1974, while the finishing touches were being put on a multi-million-dollar new winery, the first varietals, labeled *Voltaire*, and a less expensive line under the *Summit* label, were introduced in 30 cities in nine states. Although the winery remains small in comparison with some California giants, its future is planned on the basis of national sales.

Dante Bagnani, who purchased the winery with his father and brother in 1937, remained on as vice president in charge of operations. The winemaker is Al Huntsinger, one of California's best-known enologists who was with Almaden for many years, and the grape procurement manager (Geyser Peak has about 300 acres but buys grapes from other growers as well) is Bob Meyer, a long-time North Coast grape expert. George A. Vare, formerly of Schlitz, is president.

The new owners also bought out the nearby Nervo Winery, with its 85 acres of vineyards, for expanded cellar space.

Souverain of Alexander Valley, Geyserville

(See Souverain Cellars Inc., Rutherford)

J. Pedroncelli Winery, Geyserville

One of the most interesting wineries in Sonoma County is that of the Pedroncelli family, which acquired the vineyards in 1927. John G. Pedroncelli, who restored the original 1904 winery to commercial production after the evil days of Prohibition, has been succeeded by his two sons, co-owners John A. Pedroncelli, general manager, and James Pedroncelli, who is in charge of sales.

Although the winery has been expanded several times, the original wood and concrete building still is in use. Two new concrete block buildings have been added for the aging of wine in small oak casks and bottles. The vineyards are being replanted extensively with emphasis on the classic varietals—Pinot noir, Cabernet Sauvignon, White Riesling, Chardonnay, and Gewurztraminer—and only grapes from the family's and neighboring properties are crushed, giving Pedroncelli wines a definite regional character. All varietals are vintage dated.

As the demand for the Pedroncellis' wines has increased, the winery complex has grown. The facilities for temperature-controlled fermentation were doubled in 1973, along with the area for bottle aging.

Table wines available under the *J. Pedroncelli* label include:

RED: Burgundy, Cabernet Sauvignon, Sonoma Red, Pinot Noir, Zinfandel, Gamay Beaujolais;

WHITE: Chablis, Johannisberg Riesling, Sonoma White, Chardonnay, Chenin Blanc, Gewurztraminer;

ROSÉ: Sonoma Rosé and Zinfandel Rosé.

Trentadue Winery, Geryserville

This winery is at once new and old-fashioned. Although the first commercial crush was in 1969, and the present winery and tasting room were not completed until 1974, Leo Trentadue had been raising grapes and selling them to other wineries for many years. At the same time, he always made wine for his family, something he picked up from his father, Joseph, an Italian farmer.

By the late sixties Trentadue had nearly 150 acres planted to prime varietals, and with the encouragement of some other winemakers who had been buying grapes from his two vineyards, he decided to take the plunge. Production still is somewhat limited, and growth will be slow and carefully planned—to a goal of about 30,000 cases a year by 1980 and a maximum total of 50,000 cases eventually. Grapes not selected for Trentadue wines continue to be sold.

The winery is a family enterprise: Leo is viticulturist and wine-maker; his wife, Evelyn, is chief labeler and tasting room hostess; their oldest daughter, Annette, is bottler and labeler; Victor, their teenage son, is a farm hand and cellarman, and the youngest, Lisa Ann, helps fill special orders.

Trentadue says he strives to make wines of the old-fashioned, "gutsy" type, "high in tannin, alcohol by volume and individuality." The vineyards are planted to Cabernet Sauvignon, Zinfandel, Petite Sirah, Gamay, Carignane, Early Burgundy, Semillon, French Colombard, Chenin Blanc and Sauvignon Vert. All the wines are bottled as varietals, with the exception of a Burgundy.

Italian Swiss Colony, Asti

The origin of Italian Swiss Colony is in great part the story of Andrea Sbarboro, who came to San Francisco from Italy in the early eighteen fifties as a youngster to work in his brother's grocery store. Twenty years later, by working hard and saving, he bought his own store and turned builder and financier.

In 1881 he founded the Italian Swiss Agricultural Colony with the purpose of aiding Italian and Swiss immigrants to settle in their new land. Many of these were vineyardists by trade and a 1500 acre tract was chosen in Sonoma County, suitable for the planting of vines. The land was named Asti after the town of that name in Piedmont, Italy. Each immigrant was provided with room, board, and wages, in return for which a contribution was expected toward building up an equity in the land and eventually becoming an independent farmer. The immigrants objected to the last condition; they were willing to work, but not to take a chance. Sbarboro decided to oper-ate Asti privately. He set the immigrants to work, planting vines with the idea of growing and selling grapes. The price of the latter soon dropped below the cost of production. It was then decided to press the grapes into wine. The first crush was a disaster owing to carelessness in handling; the wine turned to vinegar.

Asti, so far, had proved a failure, but Sbarboro did not give up. He put Pietro Rossi, a San Francisco druggist who had studied wine making in Italy, in charge of the winery. This was in 1888. The first wines Rossi produced were of good quality but the market price offered for them was unprofitable. The Colony then decided to market its wines direct and set up agencies throughout the country and abroad. Italian Swiss Colony finally came into its own. The fame of its wines soon spread and many medals were received in the United States and Europe and even in the original Asti, in Piedmont.

Sbarboro built a sumptuous mansion at Asti and, being a great practical joker, equipped the gardens with a sprinkler system, copied after the one at Hellbrun in Salzburg. The purpose was not so much to sprinkle his plants, but his guests. The grounds of the estate became a maze of booby traps for the unsuspecting.

With the death of Pietro Rossi, thrown from his horse in 1911, one of the great figures of the Colony passed away. Management of the winery was taken over by his twin sons, Edmund and Robert Rossi, who had been taught the art of wine making by their father. Andrea Sbarboro, who among his other duties headed the Italian-American Bank in San Francisco, remained in charge of the Colony's promotion.

Prohibition was the last enemy to strike at Italian Swiss Colony. Sbarboro proclaimed endlessly that Prohibition was not the road to temperance and appeared before Congress in Washington to protest against this threat to man's liberty of action. But he realized that he was fighting a losing battle. He retired from the wine business and in 1923 he died, partly out of disgust, it is said, that his beloved Asti was bottling grape juice. It was, however, by selling grapes and grape juice that Asti was kept going during Prohibition. When Repeal came, the Rossi twins lost no time in reviving the Colony's wine industry and within a few years Italian Swiss had once again become one of the country's leading wineries.

The "experiment that nearly failed" was finally crowned with solid success. During the second World War Italian Swiss Colony was sold to National Distillers Products Corporation who owned it until April 1953 when it was purchased for a record figure by the Petri family, already well established in the wine industry. The next year the Petris also acquired from National Distillers the popular *Lejon* and *Hartley* Brandy labels and several months later the *Lejon* Vermouth brands. Under the Petri direction *Italian Swiss Colony* and its allied brands continued to grow and expand.

Today the *Italian Swiss Colony* labels are owned by United Vintners Inc., a subsidiary of Heublein Inc. United is said to account for over 25% of the U.S. wine industry volume.

Italian Swiss Colony largely produces generic and varietal wines under the *Colony* label, and also aperitif and dessert wines. The *Tipo* red Chianti is familiar to many, in its straw-covered, flask-shaped bottle. In addition there are other company specialties such as Cappella, a Vino Rosso type.

The well-known *Lejon** Vermouths, both dry and sweet, are now produced by United Vintners, as are the *G. & D.*† Vermouths sold in the East.

Italian Swiss Colony did much for what has become a popular pastime for the public, the touring of a winery. It is said that over 300,000 people a year now visit the Italian Swiss Colony's comfortable and attractive tasting room at Asti and tour the winery buildings. Near the ivy-covered winery is the original El Carmelo Chapel built by vineyard workers in the shape of a huge wine keg. Next door, a new Roman Catholic church has been built on property donated by I.S.C.

MENDOCINO COUNTY

Although this large coastal county produced a great deal of wine in years past (certainly more than the government ever knew about during Prohibition), the amount of good quality wine had dimin-

* Named after Lee Jones, a famed figure in the wine industry.
† From Gambarelli & Davitto.

ished until the 1960s, when plantings of premium varietals began to accelerate in old or abandoned vineyards and in some new areas. Winemaking had retained its vitality in the Ukiah and Redwood Valley neighborhoods, but it has been in recent years that good vines were put down again in the Anderson Valley around Booneville, a section once so populated with semi-skilled country winemakers it was called, aptly, "Vinegar Ridge." Now, wines of unusual quality are produced from grapes grown near Philo north of Booneville.

Husch Vineyards was founded in 1971 by a young couple, Tony Husch, who chucked a career as a city planner to plant 20 acres and become a winemaker, and his wife, Gretchen, a talented artist. Among their four wines is an excellent Pinot Noir that has some national distribution. Just down the road Deron and Pamela Edmeades, another young couple recently immigrated to the Anderson Valley, tend 40 acres of vineyard and have made wine in their small Edmeades Vineyards winery since 1972.

The vineyards of Mendocino County are the farthest north in California's North Coast region, although technically the northernmost bonded winery in the state is that of Dr. J. R. Wittwer of Eureka, whose family makes a small amount of French Colombard from grapes grown in the Napa Valley.

Cresta Blanca Winery, Ukiah

This company bears one of the oldest and most respected names in California's vinous history, but the resemblance stops there. Cresta Blanca was founded originally in the Livermore Valley near San Francisco by Charles Wetmore, whose vineyards included cuttings from the incomparable Chateaux d'Yquem and Margaux of Bordeaux. Some of the descended vines of the Sauternes variety were eventually inherited by the Wente Bros. winery in Livermore (see there). The high point in Cresta Blanca's early days was 1889, when one of Wetmore's wines won the Grand Prix at the Paris Exposition, the first American wine so honored.

The winery at Livermore survived Prohibition, changes in ownership and corporate neglect until it declined almost out of existence. In 1970 Schenley Industries, the distilling combine that bought it in 1941, sold the name and what was left of the good will along with the Roma Wine Co. to Guild Wineries and Distilleries, the San Francisco-based growers cooperative that is the nation's third-largest producer. The new owners retained Roy W. Mineau, Cresta Blanca's winemaker for more than 30 years. The name was put on Guild's old Mendocino Grape Growers winery at Ukiah, and Cresta Blanca now opeartes under an independent management.

The table and sparkling wines are made exclusively from grapes grown by co-op members in Mendocino County, although aperitif and dessert wines are still made in the Central Valley. The new wines show that somebody cares. The table wines include seven white and seven red varietals, and all are excellent values. The growers hope that with time, patience and a national sales program, the renown of the name will be restored.

Fetzer Vineyards, Ukiah

Bernard A. Fetzer and his family founded this small, 150-acre operation in 1968, in the seemingly inhospitable semi-wilderness north of Ukiah. Within two years Fetzer wines had earned a solid reputation among connoisseurs. In the words of the owners:

"In this far-north region the vine must put forth maximum effort to survive. The result is wine of much character and finesse. The Fetzer estate is a two-mile long strip of land, canyoned into the slopes of the Pacific Coast Range. The vineyards cover the gravelly benches above Seward and Forsythe Creeks—part of the headwaters of the Russian River. The wines, all vintage and mostly estate bottled, are produced, cellared and bottled at the winery."

The winemaker and general manager now is John Fetzer, eldest of 11 children ("We have a built-in labor source," he said. "I think Mom and Dad planned it that way."), and his younger brother, James, is the vineyard manager. Most of the other children are involved in the operation, including sister Patty, who does everything from bookkeeping to running the labeling line.

All aging is in small casks, 80 per cent Arkansas oak. About 75 per cent of the vineyard is in Cabernet Sauvignon, planted in unforgiving, rocky soil that yields an average of only two tons an acre.

Bernard Fetzer, who is in the timber business, started making wine as a hobby in 1965 in the horse barn of the ranch he bought in 1957. After the commercial venture started three years later, the Fetzers pooled their own talents and labor to design and build an attractive but efficient plant in what they have transformed into a cool oasis at the end of a hot canyon.

The winery remains small, with a capacity of about 60,000 gallons, but the wines, four whites and five reds (including several special lot Zinfandels), all vintage dated, are widely available.

Parducci Wine Cellars, Ukiah

This winery is located north of Ukiah and is owned and operated by three generations of the Parducci family. More than half a century of winemaking experience has gone into the growing success of this enterprise.

While the Parduccis originated in Lucca, Italy, Adolph B. Parducci was born in Santa Clara County. As a youngster, however, he went back to the land of his forefathers where he worked in the vineyards, returning to this country at the age of seventeen. In 1918 he founded the Parducci Wine Cellars near Cloverdale in Sonoma County but later, wishing for more space, he moved northwards to Mendocino County finding the suitable location he had been seeking near Ukiah. Here he established his vineyards and in 1931 began construction of the present Parducci Wine Cellars. The winery, surrounded by vineyards, is located in a charming little valley just off the Redwood Highway.

Adolph B. Parducci now is retired and has been succeeded by his sons, John and George, the former being president and winemaker and the latter secretary-treasurer. The third and fourth generations of the family are active in the business.

The usual generic table wines are produced but in recent years the accent has been increasingly placed on the dry varietals. These include Cabernet, Gamay Beaujolais, Pinot Noir and Zinfandel in the reds and Chardonnay, French Colombard, Chenin Blanc, Flora, Semillon and Sylvaner in the whites. Bottle fermented sparkling wines are also featured, including Champagne, both *Brut* and *Extra Dry,* Pink or Rosé Champagne and the inevitable Sparkling Burgundy. Aperitif and dessert wines, including dry and sweet vermouth, are available for the retail trade.

As late as 1972 most of the wine still was sold at the winery, but as the national reputation of Parducci wines grew, so did demand. Family-owned vineyards that first produced wines in 1967 have been expanded, modern new equipment has been installed and a large new warehouse and bottling facility was completed in 1974 in the vineyards near the old stone winery.

Weibel Champagne Vineyards, Redwood Valley

(See Weibel Inc., Mission San Jose)

B. *NAPA VALLEY—SOLANO DISTRICT*

This famous district is formed by the two counties bearing those names, with Napa yielding some of the finest of all California table wines.

From a viticultural point of view Napa County and Napa Valley are interchangeable terms, for it is from the valley and its bordering

hillsides that the county's famed wines originate. Only the Mayacamas Mountains separate Napa Valley from that of Sonoma, which
it parallels. Napa possesses its own romantic name, for in the Indian
language it is said to mean "plenty." Napa is indeed the "Valley of
Plenty," one of abundant beauty and fertility. Even in ancient times
wild grapes are said to have grown here in profusion.

The Napa River which flows through the valley empties, like its
Sonoma neighbor, into the waters of San Pablo Bay, connecting with
that of San Francisco. Dominating the valley to the north thrones
Mt. St. Helena, allegedly christened after that saint by the Princess
Helena Gagarin, wife of the one-time Russian Governor of Siberia
and of the Russian Northern Pacific Colonies and daughter of the
Czar of all the Russias.

As mentioned earlier, a staggering number of new wineries were
established, or old ones revitalized, in the late 1960s and early 1970s.
A good portion of them were in or near the Napa Valley, which
had become a Mecca for wine snobs as well as serious students of
the subject.

Some small Napa Valley wineries have histories stretching back
into the last century or the early part of this one, such as J. Mathews
in Napa, established by a Portuguese immigrant in 1878 and purchased by Orange County businessman Kenneth E. Nelson in 1969;
Sutter Home Winery at St. Helena, a family-owned operation
founded in 1890; and the Pope Valley Winery, started in 1910 but
acquired by the James Devitt family in 1972.

The year 1969 also saw the establishment of the Vintage Winery
at the Vintage 1870 boutique center in Yountville and Lyncrest
Vineyards near St. Helena, which first sold its grapes to other
winemakers but now is making wines of its own. In 1970 Cuvaison
was founded near Calistoga, and already it has undergone changes
in ownership. Carneros Creek Vineyards at Napa, Caymus Vineyards at Rutherford and the unique and beautiful Diamond Creek
Vineyards near Calistoga, owned by an energetic couple, Al Broun-
stein and his wife, Boots, were bonded in 1972. In 1973 Chateau

Chevalier on Spring Mountain and Joseph Phelps Vineyards near St. Helena, namesake of a Denver contractor who put it together with a huge investment, were established.

The tendency for every enophile with a little loose capital to become a vigneron reached something of a plateau when the economic bubble burst during the 1974 harvest, and some observers believed the proliferation of new wineries would level off, leaving those with patience, fortitude, talent and a good reputation already established to muddle through the uncertain second half of the decade.

NAPA COUNTY—UPPER NAPA VALLEY

Chateau Montelena, Calistoga

The early wines of this new winery in the shadow of Mt. St. Helena were very good, and carried the promise that Chateau Montelena would be an important, albeit small producer. Although the present operation was not established until 1968, the history of the winery goes back to 1882 when the impressive stone "chateau" was built as part of a large country estate north of Calistoga.

In 1968 Lee Paschich purchased the property and restored the nineteenth-century building to its use as a winery. He planted 100 acres of Cabernet Sauvignon and Zinfandel, and over the years modern new equipment and small European and American cooperage were installed. In 1972 a new partnership was formed and Mike Grgish, an experienced Napa Valley winemaker, was hired. The first crush of Chardonnay and Johannisberg Riesling grapes grown in the Napa and Alexander Valleys was made in 1972, Cabernet and Zinfandel from the chateau vineyards were added the following year, and plans called for the addition of Gamay Rosé to the line. By 1975 the capacity had reached 100,000 gallons.

The former owner of the estate who used it as a country home had built an oriental park complete with a five-acre lake, islands, Chinese pavillions and bridges and a dragon-eyed junk, none of which has much to do with winemaking but adds to the atmosphere. Visits are by appointment only.

Schramsberg Vineyards, Calistoga

This is the successor to the vineyards and winery of Jacob Schram, made famous in literature by Robert Louis Stevenson.

Jacob Schram (or Schramm, as he first spelled it) was a German barber from Johannisberg on the Rhine who did very well in his trade. In 1862 he bought the Mt. Diamond property on the steep hillsides just south of Calistoga, built himself a winery and a mansion, and had a number of cellars dug deep in the mountain. His Schramsberg wines became celebrated, not only in California but in far-off places and are said to have been served at the Carlton Club in London.

The Robert Louis Stevensons, while honeymooning on nearby Mt. St. Helena, visited the Schrams and Stevenson related his impressions in the chapter entitled "Napa Wine" of his *Silverado Squatters.* Fanny Stevenson was entertained by the opulent Mrs. Schram on the veranda of the big house, decorated with a wondrous collection of stuffed birds, while Stevenson and his host tasted one wine after the other in the hillside cellars. He tasted them all, Red Schramsberger and White, Burgundy Schramsberger and Schramsberger Hock. There were varietal wines also and Stevenson dwells on the bouquet of Schramsberger Golden Chasselas. The charm of these wines must have been as great as that of their names, which roll so savorously over the tongue.

After Jacob Schram's death the property was inherited by his son Herman. Prohibition rendered Schramsberg useless for wine making and it was sold to a firm of investment speculators. In 1921 it was acquired by Captain Raymond C. Naylor, who used it as a summer home, and in 1940 Schramsberg was purchased by John Gargano, who had started his California Champagne Company in the early thirties. Gargano had great plans for Schramsberg, but was not able to carry them out because of illness, and he passed away in the beginning of 1952. In 1951 the Schramsberg property was purchased by Douglas Pringle who revived the *Schramsberg* label.

In 1957, the winery was designated by the State of California as a Historical Landmark.

The present history of the winery began in 1965 when Jack L. Davies, an enophile with experience, ambition and dedication, purchased Schramsberg and began its full restoration. Since he wished to produce only bottle-fermented sparkling wines of premium quality, he replanted the vineyards above the winery to Chardonnay and Pinot noir, the principal varieties of France's Champagne District.

The Champagne making itself is carried out in the classical method, with wines aged on the yeast up to four years, depending on variety, before rebottling. The tunnels maintain an even 58-degree temperature throughout the year and provide an excellent environment for bottle-aging. Scramsberg Champagnes normally are vintage-dated and are finished to a very dry edge, bearing no indication of degree of sweetness on the labels.

The wines available under the *Schramsberg* name are as follows:
Blanc de Blancs—a medium-bodied cuvée of Chardonnay and Pinot blanc (offered in regular, reserve and nature grades);

Cuvée de Gamay—a light, tart, pink sparkling wine of the Napa Gamay, and Pinot noir;

Blanc de Noir—a rare wine (white Champagne of the red Pinot noir grape with some Chardonnay), fuller-bodied than the Blanc de Blancs, with the distinctive aroma of Pinot noir;

Cremant—a dessert Champagne, demi-sec, produced of the Flora grape and "creaming" with about half the effervescence of standard Champagne.

Sterling Vineyards, Calistoga

In late 1971 construction was started on what was to become one of the most modern and imposing wineries in the upper Napa Valley, a 35,000 square-foot crushing, storage and bottling facility on a hillside overlooking the 400 acres of Sterling Vineyards.

According to Peter L. Newton, president, and Michael Stone, vice president of the owning corporation, the winery eventually would process about 250,000 gallons per year, all from prime varietals and all vintage-dated.

Sterling Vineyards started with a small temporary crushing operation in 1969. The huge new winery, gleaming white like a Moorish castle brooding over the valley and reached by an aerial tram, was opened to the public in mid-1973. It became such a tourist attraction that in 1974 construction was undertaken of a large new visitors facility with more air-conditioned tasting rooms and special areas for private parties.

The 1969 Merlot was the first estate-bottled Merlot, a variety normally blended in the red wines of Bordeaux, in California. Other wines released by the end of 1974 were Merlot Primeur, Cabernet Sauvignon, Zinfandel, Blanc de Sauvignon, Pinot Chardonnay, Gewurztraminer and Chenin Blanc.

Winemaker R. W. Forman also is a vice president of the company, and T. E. Child is the vineyard manager.

Beringer Vineyards, St. Helena

This famous winery, known also as the Los Hermanos Vineyards, was continuously operated as a family concern since its founding in 1876 by the brothers Frederick and Jacob L. Beringer.

Jacob Beringer had learned the art of winemaking in his native Rheingau in Germany as well as in France and when he came to this country his one ambition was to establish a winery and vineyards of his own, such as he had known in Europe. He found the ideal location for his purpose while on a visit to St. Helena and he persuaded his brother Frederick who was already settled in New York in business to come out to California and join him in his project. The result was the founding of the Beringer Brothers' vineyards and winery and of a great name in the California wine industry.

The "Los Hermanos" name was aptly bestowed on the firm by a close friend of the Beringer brothers, Señor Tiburcio Parrott, a Spanish gentleman of the old school who lived in a beautiful villa in St. Helena and was a well known patron of the arts.

A special feature of the winery is the maze of tunnels cut into the hill behind it. There are a thousand feet of this tunneling, originally cut out by Chinese coolies with picks. The tunnels provide an ideal storage space at a steady air conditioned temperature for the aging of wines in fine old casks of oak.

Beringer Bros. was incorporated in 1914 with the descendants of Jacob and Frederick Beringer as members. They sold out in 1971 to the Nestle Co.

Los Hermanos carries on as of old, but adapting itself to the changing times. While the Beringer policy is to market well aged wines blended so their character and quality remain continuous over the years plans are to concentrate more on the production of varietal table wines. Some 1,400 acres of new vineyards have been added to 800 already in production.

After some difficulty with adjacent property owners, construction of a large new winery facility with stainless steel fermenters and buildings to house oak cooperage was started in 1974. Winemaker Myron Nightingale expected it to be in full production in time for the 1975 vintage. Table wines include the regular types of which the Chablis and the Burgundy are the most popular. Varietals include Cabernet Sauvignon, Grignolino, Pinot Noir and Zinfandel in the reds and Johannisberg Riesling, Grey Reisling, Chenin Blanc, Fume Blanc and Chardonnay in the whites.

The usual types of aperitif and dessert wines are marketed, a specialty being Malvasia Bianca.

Beringer's proprietary red wine, Barenblut ("Blood of the Bear") has been a popular specialty.

Burgess Cellars, St. Helena

The old site of Souverain Cellars, the winery and the vineyards were purchased in 1972 by Tom Burgess after Souverain, recently acquired by Pillsbury Mills, moved from Howell Mountain to a large new facility off the Silverado Trail near Rutherford.

The original winery and vineyards were started in the 1880s by the Rossini family, who produced country wines for bulk sale. The vineyards were abandoned during Prohibition, and in 1943 Souverain founder Lee Stewart bought the property. He sold out in 1970.

The Burgesses extensively remodeled the winery, adding new equipment and expanding the oak cooperage. Nevertheless Tom Burgess says the operation will remain relatively small. "We sometimes use the following analogy as an example," he said. "How would you compare the quality of a fine gourmet dinner you prepared for six or so persons to one you cooked for a crowd of two hundred."

Eight wines are offered, made either from their own grapes or those purchased from other Napa and Sonoma County growers. They are Chardonnay, Johannisberg Riesling, Green Hungarian, Chenin Blanc, Grenache Rosé, Cabernet Sauvignon, Petite Sirah and Zinfandel.

Visitors are welcome at the winery daily.

Chappellet Vineyard, St. Helena

What at least one expert has described as "the best-looking winery built in this century" was completed and bonded just in time for the 1969 harvest by Donn Chappellet, a "dropout" who turned his back on his giant food vending machine empire in Southern California in 1967 and moved his large family to a 100-acre vineyard 1,500 feet up Pritchard Hill above the Napa Valley.

The dun-colored concrete and steel building is laid out in the form of a triangle, the winery's symbol. Chappellet and his winemaker, Joe Cafaro, bottle only four varieties—Chenin Blanc, Johannisberg Riesling, Chardonnay and Cabernet Sauvignon. The first wine released for sale, the 1968 Chenin Blanc, was made and cellared for Chappellet by friends.

The 45,000-gallon-per-year capacity winery is expected to be in full production by 1975. In the meantime those who find the earlier Chappellet Vineyard wines can count themselves fortunate.

The Christian Brothers' Champagne Cellars, St. Helena

(See The Christian Brothers, Napa)

Conradi Vineyard, St. Helena

Founded in 1967 by Art and Susie Martin, who came to the Napa Valley from the Bay Area, this winery was known for several years as Martin Spring Mountain Inc. As a result of a long dispute over the name with Spring Mountain Vineyards, owned by Michael Robbins, the Martins changed the name in 1974 to Conradi, after Peter Conradi, who started the original winery in 1886 on land that once had been part of one of General Vallejo's land grants.

In 1968 the Martins bought the ranch, reactivated the winery which had fallen to disuse, sold off most of the vineyards and began making wines from grapes purchased from other North Coast growers. They produce Zinfandel, Cabernet and Petite Sirah exclusively, with a planned capacity of about 10,000 cases a year.

Freemark Abbey Winery, St. Helena

This is both one of the oldest and one of the newest wineries in the Napa Valley—a highway landmark two miles north of St. Helena built in 1895 by Antonio Forni, out of business by the 1950's, and then recently restored to its original purpose by a partnership of seven vineyard owners and businessmen.

Freemark Abbey is well known to tourists as the location of the Hurd Candle Shop, a gourmet shop and restaurant. The winery is located in the lower story of the attractive old stone building. Charles Carpy, one of the partners, explained what's been going on there:

"All the old floors, ceilings, plumbing and electricity were replaced and new winemaking equipment installed. Our aging is done in 60-

gallon French oak barrels with the exception of Johannisberg Riesling, which is aged in 2,300-gallon American oak tanks.

"The majority of our vineyards are located in the Rutherford area, (climate) Region II . . . In all we will have about 550 acres of vineyard producing within a few years . . . Our production started in 1967 with 60 tons of grapes. In 1970 we crushed 285 tons . . . We should reach our ultimate crush in 1972 of about 400 tons."

Freemark Abbey wines now available are Pinot Chardonnay and Johannisberg Riesling, and Cabernet Sauvignon and Pinot Noir, all vintage-dated.

Freemark Abbey stuck to its 400-ton limitation, but by the end of 1974, the aging capacity of the winery had been expanded to handle about 60,000 cases, and sales were about 20,000 cases a year in 25 states. A new bottling room, laboratory and visitors facility were completed.

Beginning in 1968 Freemark Abbey made small quantities of Cabernet Sauvignon from the 15-acre vineyard of John Bosché, northwest of Rutherford. The wine turned out so well that starting in 1972, the winery acquired the entire harvest, including some Merlot, and a wine called Cabernet Bosché was marketed, the first from the 1970 vintage.

Heitz Wine Cellars, St. Helena

In less than a decade, Joseph E. Heitz built up his winery from what amounted to a modest roadside business to the point where its name is synonymous among connoisseurs with the finest California wines.

To understand the phenomenon, one must know something of Joe Heitz himself. During the war, while he was stationed in California with the Army, he became interested in wine, and after his discharge he enrolled at the University of California at Davis. He graduated in viticulture and enology, and for the next 10 years he worked as a winemaker for many of the state's leading wineries. He taught viticulture and enology at Fresno State College, and has been a wine judge at the California State Fair for many years. He and his wife, Alice, constantly taste the wines of the world at their own table and through their active membership in the Wine and Food Society.

In 1961 the Heitzes decided it was time to risk giving up the security of working for others and, in a move that required determination as well as raw nerve, they purchased a small winery just south of St. Helena which had been owned by the late Leon Brendel.

Brendel also was an interesting figure in the California wine industry. A member of a family of wine growers, he was born in the Alsace District of France and studied chemistry in France and Germany. After helping to organize a school for distillers in Switzerland, he went to Mexico at the request of the family of President Madero and became winemaker and chemist for the Madero winery and vineyards in the State of Coahuila. Following Repeal he came to California as a wine consultant. In 1949 he purchased the winery at St. Helena which he operated until his death, producing only one wine, a Grignolino marketed, appropriately enough, under the *Only One* brand.

Joe and Alice Heitz worked literally night and day to establish their new enterprise and by 1964, the Heitzes were in a position to acquire a second winery and a plot of vineyard land in a valley tucked in the foothills southeast of St. Helena. The "new" winery is a picturesque, two-story stone structure built in 1898. Heitz fitted it with new equipment and seasoned cooperage and began replanting the vineyards to top varietals.

"With our new vineyard and winery we . . . have a self-contained operation," he said, "in which we can plant the varietals we believe will ultimately yield the best wines, direct the care and training of the vines ourselves and from the grapes produce the quality of wine of which the Napa Valley is really capable.

"We will also continue to select other top quality wines and sell them under the *Heitz Cellar* label."

The Heitz children have, from the time they were too young to drink the product, been active in the family concern, with the result that during the critical days of the 1974 harvest, when his father was unexpectedly hospitalized, son David ably took over and handled the crush.

A beautiful new winery and office complex was completed adjacent to the old stone cellars and the Heitz home in 1973. Slow and orderly expansion should raise the annual production to an eventual 100,000 gallons per year—good news for the legions of Heitz fans around the country.

Heitz Cellar wines are as follows:

RED: Barbera, Burgundy, Cabernet Sauvignon (Vintage and Non-Vintage), Grignolino, Pinot Noir (Vintage), Ruby Cabernet (Vintage), Zinfandel;

* WHITE: Chablis, Chardonnay (Vintage), Johannisberg Riesling (Vintage), Pinot Blanc (Vintage).

Also featured are *"Cellar Treasure"* Tawny Port, a Dry Sherry, *Brut* and Extra Dry Champagne, Grignolino Rosé and Sparkling Burgundy.

Hanns Kornell Champagne Cellars, St. Helena

Hanns Kornell, a hard working and determined personality, represents the third generation of a family known in Germany since 1848 for their superior wines and champagnes. He attended agricultural college and worked in vineyards and wineries, acquiring experience in France and Italy as well as in his native country. With him as with every true vintner one can say that wine has always run in his blood.

When political conditions made it impossible for Hanns Kornell to remain in Germany he chose America as his new home. In 1940 he hitchhiked to California with $2.00 in his pocket but with determination in his heart. He worked at Fountaingrove in Santa Rosa, then a famous vineyard and winery. He also worked for the Gibson Wine Company in Cincinnati, Ohio, and for the American Wine Company in St. Louis, Missouri, at that time producers of the well known Cook's Champagne, where he was the winemaker and later became production manager.

His great ambition was to manage his own winery and this he accomplished in 1952 when he leased a winery in Sonoma from the Sonoma Wine Company, renaming it Hanns Kornell Cellars. By hard work and a strong inner drive he made his venture a success, so much so that in 1958 he was able to purchase the famous old Lark-mead Winery in St. Helena from Italian Swiss Colony. He had come a long way in eighteen years, from two dollars to being the proud owner of his own winery. 1958 was very special for Hanns Kornell for in that year also he married Marilouise Rossini whose grandfather had homesteaded in St. Helena.

The winery's accent is on production of bottle-fermented sparkling wines. These are carefully made, aged and bottled under Hanns Kornell's personal and untiring supervision. They include *Sehr Trocken* (German for extremely dry), *Brut, Extra Dry, Sec,* Pink (Rosé) Champagne as well as *Muscadelle du Bordelais* and Sparkling Burgundy, all marketed under the *Hanns Kornell* "Third Generation" brand. Of these the *Brut* Champagne is particularly outstanding.

The Kornells' two children are active in the family business, which has added a select brandy to the line, available at the winery.

Charles Krug Winery (C. Mondavi & Sons), St. Helena

This firm, now run by the Mondavi family, is the worthy successor to Charles Krug, a great figure in the development of the California wine industry.

Charles Krug was born in Trendelburg, Prussia, in 1825 and emigrated to America as a young man. He returned to his fatherland to take part in the democratic uprising of 1848 and on the failure of that movement returned to the United States for good. He came to California and devoted his energies to a study of viticulture with the aim of establishing his own winery and vineyards. He worked for General Vallejo and Colonel Haraszthy and became convinced of the desirability of planting European grape varieties. In 1858 he purchased some acreage of his own and made viticultural history by producing, from the grapes of John Patchett of Napa, some 1200 gallons of wine with a small cider press. This was the first wine obtained in Napa County by modern methods. The press is preserved at the Krug Ranch today, a treasured memento of its founder.

Krug built his original winery at St. Helena in 1861. The fame of his wines spread throughout the country and beyond. By 1880 the Krug Ranch was considered one of the most beautiful and productive in the Napa Valley and Krug himself was well established as a leader of the wine industry. Such men as Carl Wente and the Beringer brothers worked for him and obtained valuable experience.

After the death of Charles Krug in 1894 the Ranch was purchased by his close friend and admirer, James K. Moffitt, who used it as a country home. The winery and vineyards were leased until Prohibition forced them into a dormant period.

When Repeal came the Moffitt family was willing to sell the Ranch but only to a winemaking family capable of reviving the fame and prestige of the Krug wines. With a feeling of accomplishing this purpose the property was sold, in 1943, to Cesare Mondavi and his sons Robert and Peter.

Cesare Mondavi came to America from Ancona, Italy and his, too, is the story of successful enterprise. He first went to work in the ore mines of Minnesota. There he was chosen by a group of Italian home winemakers to select and buy grapes for them in California. He came to stay, engaging in the wine-grape shipping business expanding later to include other fruit. After Repeal he entered the winemaking field, first producing dessert type wines at the Acampo Winery in Lodi. Later he began to produce dry table wines at the Sunny St. Helena Winery in St. Helena. Anxious to concentrate on the production of premium wines the Mondavi family found in the Krug Ranch the means to achieve their goal. Having built up the business with the help of his sons to the present renewed fame of the Krug wines Cesare died in 1959 at the age of 76.

Following his death, Cesare's sons, Peter and Robert, continued to operate the winery. Both graduated from Stanford University and both studied viticulture and enology under University of California scientists. Robert left the family firm to establish his own winery at Oakville in 1966, and Peter now administers Charles Krug as vice president, while their mother, Mrs. Rosa Mondavi, retains the title of president.

Since 1943 the Mondavis have renovated the Krug plant at great expense, modernizing the winery and cellars and re-equipping the buildings. In the vineyards the older wines were gradually replaced and always with the finer varietals. A new glass-lined tank and bottling room were added. These glass-lined tanks, in essence huge bottles, can hold approximately 1,375,000 gallons of wine. The purpose is to be able to bottle the wines when they have received the necessary wood age. It has always been the opinion of the Mondavis that just as much damage can be done to the wine if it is allowed to remain in the wood too long as there would be if it were taken out too soon.

In addition to the glass-lined tanks a new method of bottling has been instituted with certain technical advantages making for better wines. Both these innovations are big steps forward insuring maximum quality.

The main accent of the Krug-Mondavi production is on premium table wines although a few aperitif and dessert wines, including a Tinta Madeira Port, are matured and bottled at the winery to round out the line. A number of less expensive wines are marketed under the *CK Mondavi label* (not to be confused with *Robert Mondavi* wines).

Charles Krug remains the featured brand* for the premium wines. The usual generic table wines are produced; the list of the varietals follows:

RED: Cabernet Sauvignon, Gamay Beaujolais, Pinot Noir, Zinfandel;

* No connection with the Krug Champagne of France.

WHITE: Dry Semillon, Blanc Fumé, White Pinot (from 70–75% Chenin blanc and 30–25% Pinot blanc grapes) on the sweet side, Chenin Blanc (from 100% Chenin blanc grapes) on the dry side, Pinot Chardonnay, Traminer, Gewurztraminer, Sylvaner, Grey Riesling and Johannisberger Riesling.

The winery also produces a Vin Rosé and Moscato Canelli, a lightly sweet Muscat.

The Mondavis publish an informative and popular quarterly "Uncorked and poured from time to time by Charles Krug Winery" entitled *Bottles and Bins,* Francis L. Gould, Editor. It gives news about the winery, about the wine industry in general and supplies some very useful and tasty recipes.

Louis M. Martini, St. Helena

The wines produced by Louis Martini rate among the finest of California. Born in Pietra Ligure on the Italian Riviera, Louis M. Martini came to San Francisco as a boy and first assisted his father Agostino Martini, in the latter's mussels, clams and fish business. In 1906, the year of the earthquake, the decision was made to enter the wine making field. A small plant was built in San Francisco, some forty by seventy-five feet, the modest forerunner of the modern and imposing Louis Martini winery in St. Helena of today.

Louis Martini returned to Italy to study winemaking and then returned to California to practice the knowledge he had acquired. He worked for various winemakers, including the famous Secundo Guasti, founder of the Italian Vineyard Company at Guasti. Later Louis Martini built a winery and distillery at Kingsburg in southern San Joaquin Valley for the production of sweet wines and brandy. His ambition, however, had always been directed toward producing premium quality table wines. When he sold his Kingsburg plant for a good price he settled in St. Helena to fulfill his ambition, armed with the necessary know-how, drive and capital.

The St. Helena winery was built in 1933 and Louis Martini successively acquired other vineyard complexes. The Napa, or La Loma vineyard, part of the former Rancho Rincon de los Carneros, lies on the rolling, gravelly slopes of the southern end of the Mayacamas range, southwest of the town of Napa. It specializes in Cabernet Sauvignon, Pinot noir and Zinfandel vines.

Most famous, however, is the vineyard formerly called Goldstein, planted in the early eighteen eighties and by Martini renamed Monte Rosso after its red volcanic soil. It is situated at an altitude of over 1000 feet on the crest of the Mayacamas mountains dividing Napa and Sonoma counties. In this cool climate wine grape varieties attain top quality. The Monte Rosso vines include Cabernet Sauvignon, Barbera, Zinfandel in the reds and White Riesling, Gewurztraminer, Sylvaner, Chardonnay, Folle blanche and Semillon in the whites. The wines produced from these grapes are truly "Mountain Wines" and usually carry that designation on the label.

In the early 1960's three additional ranches were added to the Martini holdings. One, on the Russian River bench south of Healdsburg in Sonoma County, was planted predominantly to Pinot noir, Chardonnay, Cabernet Sauvignon, Merlot, Malbec and Gamay. A second, in the Carneros District south of Napa, has been planted entirely to Pinot noir. The third is in Chiles Valley five miles east of St. Helena (at an elevation of 900 feet).

Louis M. Martini died in 1974. His son, Louis P. Martini, has replaced him as president and general manager. A grandson, Michael Martini, is studying enology and will take an active interest in the business, as will his brother, Peter.

Wines are marketed under the *Louis M. Martini* brand and include the following varietal table wines, all vintage:

RED: Cabernet Sauvignon available in especially fine years as Cabernet Sauvignon Special Selection, Mountain Pinot Noir, Mountain Barbera, Mountain Zinfandel, Mountain Merlot;

WHITE: Johannisberg Riesling, Mountain Gewurztraminer, Mountain Folle Blanche, Mountain Riesling (from Sylvaner grapes),

Mountain Dry Chenin Blanc, Mountain Pinot Chardonnay;
ROSÉ: Mountain Gamay Rosé (from Gamay grapes), Mountain Vin Rosé.

The red and white varietals also are available in magnums.

Generic table wines are also produced: Mountain Red Wine, Mountain Claret, Mountain Chianti and Mountain Burgundy in the reds and Mountain White Wine and Mountain Chablis in the whites.

Three aperitif and dessert wines are available: Pale Dry Sherry (very pale and very dry, of the *Fino* type and aged according to the Solera system), Cream Sherry, Tawny Port (limited quantity only).

Not generally known is that Louis Martini also produces a slightly effervescent wine, Moscato Amabile, made from the Muscat of Alexandria grape, light, delicate and quite sweet. It can only be obtained directly from the winery and should be stored in the refrigerator and consumed early to avoid spoiling.

Also available only from the winery direct are small quantities of very special vintage table wines, the vintages varying naturally as time progresses. This gourmet listing of Martini's "Older Vintages and Special Selection Wines" will include: Cabernet Sauvignon, Pinot Noir, Zinfandel, Barbera, Johannisberg Riesling, Pinot Chardonnay, Gewurztraminer. In each case the vintage year is indicated as well as the year in which the wine was bottled.

Nichelini Vineyards, St. Helena

When Anton Nichelini established his winery in 1890 in the Chiles Valley southeast of St. Helena, he brought years of experience to his new venture. A native of Switzerland, he went to France at an early age to learn the art of winemaking, and he worked for one of California's largest wineries after immigrating to the United States.

Nichelini Vineyards always has been a family affair. It was operated after 1933 by Anton's son William, and since the latter's death in 1959, by Anton's grandson, James. A great-grandson, James Jr., already works in the vineyard.

James Nichelini Sr. had been making wine since he was 17 years old. Although he has replanted much of the vineyard and has started an expansion program at the winery, the original plant built by his grandfather still is in use. Today, the Nichelini property yields Cabernet Sauvignon, Gamay, Petite Sirah, Zinfandel, Chenin blanc, Flora, Palomino and Sauvignon vert grapes.

Table wines available under the *Nichelini Vineyard* label are as follows:

RED: Burgundy, Cabernet, Sauvignon, Gamay, Zinfandel;

WHITE: Chablis, Chenin Blanc, Sauvignon Vert;

ROSÉ: Vin Rosé (of Zinfandel grapes).

In addition, Nichelini Vineyards markets a Dry Sherry and a Port.

Stony Hill Vineyard, St. Helena

Some seven hundred feet above the floor of the Napa Valley, on the steep hillsides between Spring and Diamond mountains, lies the Stony Hill Vineyard, the name of which speaks for itself. The vineyard, some 28 acres, is planted mainly to three varieties, all white: Chardonnay, White Riesling and Gewurztraminer.

Frederick H. McCrea, now retired from his position as vice president and manager of the San Francisco office of McCann-Erickson, Inc., an internationally known advertising agency, long had the ambition to see what he could do about producing good wines in small quantities. He purchased the Stony Hill property in 1943 and built a small but modern winery in 1951. The wine is fermented in small cooperage, and much of it is held two years before sale.

For many years McCrea crushed only a small portion of his grapes, selling the bulk of his harvest to other winemakers. All grapes from the vineyard now are crushed and bottled under the *Stony Hill* label. All three of the wines offered are 100% of the variety named, and carry the vintage date as well as the Napa Valley appellation of origin.

Spring Mountain Vineyards, St. Helena

Michael Robbins, a San Francisco businessman and dedicated enophile, established his cellars in a restored Victorian house north of St. Helena, and began planting prime varieties in the late 1960s. The first wines, from purchased grapes and later his own, were fermented by other winemakers and then cellared, finished and bottled in the basement of the Robbins home. They held great promise, and wine lovers throughout the country watched the progress with happy anticipation.

They weren't disappointed. The Cabernet Sauvignon, Chardonnay and Sauvignon Blanc of various vintages were consistent prize winners and were much sought after. The only complaint seemed to be that even after Spring Mountain was making its own wines, supplies were limited. Fortunately, that problem was being solved.

In April of 1974 the Robbinses purchased the old Tiburcio Parrott estate on Spring Mountain Road, which had been called "Miravalle" for its view of the Napa Valley. Patterned after the "Rhine House" built by the Beringers nearby, Miravalle was constructed in the late nineteenth century, and Parrott made wines of some distinction.

The property purchased by Spring Mountain included 265 acres, of which 100 will be planted. Robbins said the winery will retain a 105-acre parcel near Rutherford, and possibly the Soda Creek Ranch, both of which were planted and in production. The Victorian house that adorned the Spring Mountain label was sold, and early in 1975 the Robbinses moved to the Parrott estate.

Yverdon Vineyards, St. Helena

Named for the Swiss village where the founder's grandmother was born, Yverdon vineyards was established in 1970 by Fred Aves, a Los Angeles manufacturer and hobby winemaker who had been growing grapes near Calistoga for a number of years, and his son, Russell.

The first crush was in 1971 from grapes grown at the Calistoga ranch, where 90 acres are planted to Cabernet Sauvignon, Gamay Beaujolais, Johannisberg Riesling and Chenin Blanc. Gewurztraminer was planted in 1972 at the 20-acre home vineyard near the winery on Spring Mountain near St. Helena, along with some Merlot.

The well-equipped modern winery had reached a fermenting capacity of more than 25,000 gallons by 1975, with room for storage of twice that much, assuring fairly wide availability of Yverdon wines, which have been very well received.

Beaulieu Vineyard, Rutherford

It was just before the turn of the century that a young Frenchman, Georges de Latour, came to California, desirous of producing table wines comparable in quality and character to the finer ones of his native France. He had heard much about California's favorable climate and soil and he came to see for himself. He stemmed from a family well known in both the Bordeaux and Burgundy regions and was already familiar with many of the problems of viticulture and of the difficult art of winemaking. He was, besides, gifted with an exceptionally fine taster's palate, an attribute of primary importance to all those engaged in the wine business, and especially in the producing end of it.

Georges de Latour traveled through California searching for the ideal location suited to his purpose and found what he sought in the Rutherford area in the Napa Valley. It was here, in 1900, that he founded the Beaulieu* estate and vineyards, as he named them so appropriately.

For some forty years Georges de Latour devoted his energies to the production of the finest wines the favored climate and soil of the Napa Valley were capable of yielding. He proved himself eminently successful in his endeavor and established a solid reputation for the Beaulieu wines throughout the United States and abroad.

During Prohibition the winery continued to operate, producing

---

* Meaning Beautiful Place.

sacramental wines, to which a part of the Beaulieu industry is still actively devoted. Beaulieu is one of the few wineries in California where the accent in wines and wine production is very distinctly inspired by the French taste; the whole atmosphere is that of *"la belle France,"* completely at home in the Napa Valley.

After the death of Georges de Latour in 1940, Madame de Latour presided over Beaulieu in her husband's place. Known to so many for her grace and charm, she had become the *"grande dame"* of California viticulture. With her demise, in 1951, another great figure had passed on.

Today Beaulieu is owned by Heublein Inc., the huge firm that has bought so many of California's wineries.

The fine reputation earned by Beaulieu wines over the years is largely the result of a happy blending between the traditional subtleties of French taste and know-how with modern California techniques, all combined in the person of Andre Tchelistcheff, the head winemaker from 1938 until his retirement in 1973. As is noted elsewhere in this book, Tchelistcheff was responsible for the development of a number of other premium wineries, and now enjoys the distiction of being the dean of California enologists, and perhaps of winemakers of the New World.

His son, Dimitri, is now Beaulieu's technical director; Theo Rosenbrand is cellarmaster and Thomas Selfridge is enologist. Legh F. Knowles is managing director and vice president.

Beaulieu is managed independently, and despite some expansion and change, the early fears of tremendously increased output and dilution of quality appear to have been unjustified during the first half-dozen years after the Heublein takeover.

The brand name under which all wines are marketed is *Beaulieu Vineyard*. As some have difficulty in pronouncing the name, the labels also carry the letters *B V,* and it is by this name that the wines are also widely known. All table wines are labeled with the Napa Valley appellation of origin and with the exception of Beaurosé and Grenache Rosé are estate bottled. The back label indicates exactly from which grapes the wine has been made, the varietals being mostly 100%.

An extensive line of high-quality white and red table wines is available, the most elegant (and expensive) being the Chardonnay and Cabernet Sauvignon Private Reserve. In 1974 BV released an unusual special bottling of Johannisberg Riesling Spatlese.

In recent years Beaulieu has started to produce and market sparkling wines, all bottle fermented. These are the *Beaulieu* (*B V*) Champagnes, *Brut* and *Extra Dry* and the *Rouge* or Sparkling Burgundy.

Beaulieu also markets aperitif and dessert wines matured in small oak casks including the *B V* Sherries (Pale Dry, regular, medium dry, and Cream), *B V* Port and *B V* Muscat de Frontignan.

All of the varietal table wines of Beaulieu and their sparkling wines carry the vintage year on the labeling and many an older *B V* vintage table wine has become a connoisseur's item.

Franciscan Vineyards, Rutherford

Although founded with great fanfare and ambition in 1971, it was not until October of 1974, after the firm had been reorganized with 40 shareholders, that its first wines were released.

The contemporary redwood winery is located just north of Rutherford amid 50 acres of company-owned vines. Another 200 acres are being cultivated in other parts of the Napa Valley. The winemaker and enologist is Leonard A. Berg, a Davis graduate with a dozen years of experience in the field.

The first wines emphasized whites, with nine including a sweet Muscat Canelli, compared with four reds. The winery also produces an inexpensive line of jug wines under the *Friar's Table* label.

Franciscan Vineyards said it hopes to reach an ultimate capacity of 1,300,000 gallons, making it comparable in size to Beaulieu nearby, and to produce a complete line of aperitif, dessert and sparkling wines as well as table wines.

Inglenook Vineyard Company, Rutherford

The great vinecovered stone winery of Inglenook lies in Rutherford, right in the heart of the Napa Valley. Beaulieu (see there) is its immediate neighbor.

Founder of Inglenook was that colorful Finnish seafarer, fur trader and wine grower, Captain Niebaum.

Gustave Ferdinand Nybom (later Americanized to Niebaum) was born in Helsinki, Finland, in 1842, at that time under Russian domination. He went to sea as a boy and received his master's papers when only nineteen. Two years later he had his own command and in 1864 sailed for Alaska, then also part of the Russian Empire.

For three years he ranged Alaska, the Aleutian Chain of Islands and the Asiatic shore as far as Kamchatka, bartering for furs and acquainting himself thoroughly with the region. Negotiations by the United States for the purchase of Alaska had been started and Captain Niebaum realized that America would have economic as well as political interests in the territory. He made full use of his opportunities and amassed a vast collection of seal skins and other valuable furs. When the sale of Alaska to the United States became an accomplished fact in March 1867 Captain Niebaum lost no time in loading his precious furs aboard a ship, bound for San Francisco. He was no more than twenty-six when he sailed through the Golden Gate, the owner of a cargo worth well over half a million dollars.

Captain Niebaum's knowledge of the seal habitat was invaluable to the Alaska Commercial Company, organized to obtain exclusive fur sealing rights in the Alaskan waters, and he became their youngest partner. The company proved so successful that it paid the United States Government considerably more in rights than the total cost of the Alaskan purchase.

The Captain was now ready for a less rigorous mode of life and as Mrs. Niebaum did not share his love for the sea he turned his thoughts to the land and to an enterprise that both could enjoy. On various trips that he had made to Europe on behalf of the

Alaskan company he had become increasingly interested in viticulture and winemaking. He had visited many of the European wine growing districts and had collected a large number of books on the subject. His hobby finally became his life's destiny. With enough time and money to accomplish his purpose he decided to attempt producing in California wines comparable to Europe's finest.

After a thorough search for the most suitable location Captain Niebaum purchased in 1879 a portion of the old Mexican Caymus Rancho grant, extending from Rutherford up to the slopes of Mount St. John, highest peak of the Mayacamas range. The property had already been called Inglenook (Scottish for fireside corner) by the former owner, W. C. Watson. The name appealed to Niebaum and he retained it.

Captain Niebaum devoted the following years to planning, building and planting. Further trips to the wine growing regions of Europe were made where he studied every aspect of viticulture. Cuttings of the choicest wine grape varieties were shipped home. At Inglenook he established his vineyards with the utmost care and always with due regard to the beauty of Nature. The cellars and winery were built according to the most modern specifications. Inglenook had became Captain Niebaum's ship and the vineyards his sea.

When Captain Niebaum died in 1908 Inglenook was inherited by his widow. John Daniel, the husband of Mrs. Niebaum's niece, ably directed operations for her until the advent of Prohibition. His knowledge was passed on to his son, John Daniel, Jr., who was in charge of the winery and vineyards from Repeal until he sold out to United Vintners in 1964. United became part of the Heublein empire in 1968.

Inglenook was the first winery to label many of the better known varietals as such, pioneered such wines as White Pinot,* Red Pinot,† Charbono‡ and claims to have been the first producer of Vin Rosé in California, launching it in 1935.

* Chenin Blanc, see white varietal table wines chapter.
† Pinot St. George, see red varietal table wines chapter.
‡ *Ibid.*

Inglenook produces five white and six red vintage-dated table wines, along with a Navalle Rosé, made from Gamay grapes and named after the stream that runs through the property.

In addition, since the sale to United Vintners, a new line of less expensive generics, called District Vintage Wines (not estate bottled), has been introduced. These include Burgundy, Zinfandel, Chablis and Rhine. California Grenache Rosé has been added, along with five vintage appetizer and dessert wines, three Sherries and two Ports.

A line of Navalle generic and varietal wines was recently added, and production at Inglenook, which is operated in conjunction with Italian Swiss Colony in Sonoma County, has increased astonishingly.

F. J. Miller & Co., Rutherford

It may seem unusual that this winery is included in this book, because the owner isn't exactly in the wine business. But he considers himself somewhat of a missionary for a new process for carbonating wines, and, as such, he has become one of the best known and most controversial figures in the industry.

F. Justin Miller is an Englishman who ran a plantation in the West Indies before he came to California. He studied food technology at Davis with the idea of returning to Trinidad, but after graduating in 1951 he decided to settle in the Napa Valley instead to work on his theories about carbonation. He learned that carbon dioxide introduced into liquids while they are quiescent rather than disturbed (conventional methods of artificial carbonation require violent agitation) result in greater stability. In other words, the bubbles last longer.

Miller buys and matures wine before he puts it through his "Millerway" process, which he patented in 1960. First, the wine is filtered and drawn into a pressure tank from which each bottle is filled. The bottles are placed open in small, individual cylinders, air is pumped out to prevent oxidation and carbon dioxide is introduced into the headspace at a pressure of 150 pounds per square inch. The cylinders are opened after 12 hours, the bottles are stoppered and the product is carbonated wine with about 50 pounds of pressure—roughly the same as naturally fermented Champagne. The difference is that the effervescence lasts longer after the bottle is opened, up to *sixteen days* if it is not shaken, and remains at a constant temperature.

Miller sees many other advantages to the process. Wines can be matured carefully, brought to their peak and then carbonated in a few hours. Millerway wines lack the characteristic flavor of Champagne, which he calls "yeasty" and which he believes many Americans don't enjoy. However, he adds, if a winemaker wanted the Champagne flavor, it can be achieved with the process.

His most recent invention, published in May of 1974, is a method of producing yeast-carbonated champagnes with "caged yeast," shortening the time of production and eliminating the necessity for riddling and disgorging.

Miller is not primarily interested in selling *F. J. Miller* wines, although they are available in small quantities from the winery. He is concerned with selling the process, which has not been widely accepted. He blames traditionists and the federal tax regulations which prohibit labeling machine carbonated wines as "sparkling." To back up his belief that wine producers would buy the process if they could so label their products, he has initiated legal action against the government to win that right.

The wines carbonated through the Millerway technique are sound and interesting, with true varietal flavor.

Souverain Cellars Inc., Rutherford

This corporate holding of Pillsbury Mills, including big new wineries in Napa and Sonoma Counties, bears no resemblance to the original Souverain Cellars founded in 1943 by Lee Stewart on Howell Mountain to the north. In 1970 he sold out to a consortium of new owners, staying on as a consultant. A short time later, Pillsbury acquired control of the company and sold the original winery and property to Tom Burgess of Burgess Cellars in 1972.

An attractive new winery, designed in the fashion of a gigantic barn, has been built above the Silverado Trail east of Rutherford, but production has remained limited and only four whites and four reds are made here under the direction of winemaker Philip Baxter.

A much larger output will come from Souverain of Alexander Valley, opened in 1974 in Sonoma County just south of Geyserville and an instant tourist success. Designed with large towers suggested by the hop kilns which formerly dotted the northern part of Sonoma County, the interior of the building has massive wooden beams and modern, highly-efficient winery facilities. The Chez Bacchus restaurant in the winery offers French cuisine and both Souverain wines and imported Frank Schoonmaker Selections from a company also owned now by Pillsbury. Chateau Souverain wines are produced independently of the Napa Valley winery by winemaker William Bonetti and carry their own label.

Robert Mondavi Winery, Oakville

One of the most attractive wineries in the Napa Valley is operated by Robert Mondavi, who established it in 1966.

The Mondavi family has been associated for two generations with winemaking in California, and since 1943 has owned the Charles Krug winery at St. Helena (see there). Following the death of Cesare Mondavi in 1959, Krug was operated by his sons, Peter and Robert Mondavi. Now Robert, with the assistance of his two sons, Tim and Mike, and in partnership with the Rainier Companies Inc. of Seattle, Wash., is, in the words of one associate, "working to produce the finest Napa Valley wines possible" on his own.

The winery, designed by architect Cliff May and landscaped by Thomas Church, was built with a neo-colonial motif, complete with 15th Century Spanish doors. The antique-looking adobe-colored exterior of the building conceals a modern winery where technology is married to tradition. Double-walled stainless steel tanks which allow controlled temperature fermentation contrast with small, European-made oak casks.

In 1968, the winery was expanded to accommodate as many as 400 to 500 guests for specially arranged tastings, luncheons, concerts and other events. Since 1969 the winery has held summer jazz concerts which attract up to 2,000 people who gather on the spacious lawn and listen to music under the stars.

The *Robert Mondavi Winery* varietals are Cabernet Sauvignon, Gamay, Pinot Noir, Zinfandel, Petite Sirah, Chardonnay, Chenin Blanc, Riesling (a Sylvaner), Traminer, Johannisberg Riesling and Gamay Rosé. In addition to the other whites, there is a remarkably pleasant Fume Blanc, a dry white wine of Sauvignon blanc grapes named after the Pouilly-Fume of France's upper Loire Valley, which has earned the sincerest form of flattery from other wineries: imitation.

Oakville Vineyards, Oakville

This organization was incorporated in 1969 as a descendent of Carmel Valley Wine Associates, a small company formed the year earlier to produce and market fine wines. The head of both companies is W. E. van Löben Sels, an agricultural economics graduate of the University of California and a successful Bay Area businessman. The winemaker, Peter Karl Heinz Becker, comes from a German family that has been making wine over 300 years. He joined the Carmel Valley-Oakville Vineyards venture after 11 years as plant manager and winemaker at Almaden's Cienga winery near Hollister. Also active in the day-to-day operation of the new company is Mrs. Jean van Löben Sels, the president's wife.

Oakville Vineyards has undergone extensive development and expansion in recent years, beginning at its winery and tasting room at Oakville. New vineyards have been planted, including a portion of the 1,600-acre Inglenook Ranch it acquired from the John Daniels estate. The Gustave Niebaum home, built by the founder of Inglenook, also was acquired, and here Mr. and Mrs. van Löben Sels live and entertain with great style.

The wines, produced with the help of consultant Karl Werner, formerly with the famous Schloss Vollrads in Germany's Rheingau, include Sauvignon Blanc, Sauvignon Fleur (a combination of Sauvignon Blanc and Muscat), Chenin Blanc, Gewurztraminer, Gamay Rosé, Napa Gamay, Cabernet Sauvignon and Zinfandel. Also available are "Our House" white and red wines, both pleasant, well-made generics.

NAPA COUNTY—LOWER NAPA VALLEY

The Christian Brothers (Mont La Salle Vineyards), Napa

The Mont La Salle Vineyards and Novitiate of The Christian Brothers are located high in the hills of the southwestern part of Napa County in the so-called Napa Redwoods district, some eight miles northwest from the town of Napa.

The "Brothers of the Christian Schools" as The Christian Brothers are officially called, form a congregation of the Roman Catholic Church, dedicated to the education of young men and boys. The order was founded in 1680 at Reims, France, by Jean Baptiste de la Salle, for the purpose of educating the underprivileged. Its headquarters are in Rome. Although not priests, the Brothers lead dedicated lives, having taken the vows of poverty, chastity and obedience.

The Christian Brothers first came to the United States before the middle of the nineteenth century. At present they operate one hundred and seventy-four institutes of learning in the country, such as Manhattan College in New York City, La Salle Military Academy on Long Island, St. Mel's High School in Chicago, Christian Brothers College in St. Louis and St. Mary's College at Moraga near Oakland in California.

Mont La Salle at Napa is The Christian Brother's Novitiate for

California and the Western States. Here young men are trained for the work of the congregation while a school is maintained for boys of high school age and a home for Brothers who have retired after a lifetime of service. Here also the Brothers proudly follow their wine making tradition, a heritage dating back many centuries.

In California The Christian Brothers started making wine at Martinez in 1882, at first for their own use, then for Sacramental use and later, with the growing demand by lay circles, for the public. The Brothers are sole owners of the wineries and use all net profits for the maintenance of their Novitiate at Mont La Salle, where young men are trained to carry on the educational work of the Order, and to help support the operation of various schools in the San Francisco Province.

Brother Frederick, president, and Brother Timothy, vice president and cellarmaster for many years, are assisted by other Brothers in the supervision of the wineries at Mont La Salle and St. Helena in Napa County and their distillery near Reedley in Fresno County.

The Brothers produce table and Sacramental wines in the old stone winery built at Mont La Salle in 1903. Red wines requiring long term aging are brought to the St. Helena Aging and Champagne Cellars, an old stone landmark once known as the largest stone winery in the world. After reaching their peak of maturity here in the wood they are then returned to Mont La Salle for bottling and bottle aging. The St. Helena Cellars are also the headquarters for the Brothers' champagne production. Sparkling wines are produced by the Charmat process in sixteen glistening stainless steel tanks which enable the Brothers to maintain complete scientific control. The Mt. Tivy winery is given over to the production of The Christian Brothers aperitif and dessert wines and brandy.

The production has increased to the point where The Christian Brothers have a storage capacity of over 20,000,000 gallons at various facilities. In 1972, a highly advanced "fermenting-in-the-round" operation was built south of St. Helena with a crushing and fermenting capacity of 15,000 tons (as much as 3,000,000 gallons) during the 90-day harvest season. Here 70 stainless steel tanks ranging from 3,000 to 15,000 gallons enable the Brothers to batch ferment selected grape lots.

All the Brothers' products are marked under *The Christian Brothers* brand with the exception of their Altar wines which bear the *Mont La Salle* label. In 1967, the Brothers abandoned the heavy, ornate "cathedral" bottles which had been their trademark and began marketing wines in more traditionally shaped containers.

The regular types of generic table wines and of aperitif and dessert wines, including vermouths, are available as well as (bulk fermented) sparkling wines and of course the well known *Christian Brothers* Brandy.

In 1972 a limited edition *XO Rare Reserve* brandy was introduced, containing 50% eight-year-old pot-still brandy. Several non-vintage varietals are marketed, along with an extremely popular light muscat called Chateau La Salle.

Mayacamas Vineyards, Napa

Some 2,000 feet high in the Mayacamas Mountains in the Lokoya district, near the top of Mt. Veeder, an extinct volcano, lies this small winery enthusiastically devoted to the finer things of life.

Mayacamas Vineyards was founded by Jack F. M. and Mary Catherine Taylor. A graduate of Cambridge University in England and the former president of the Shell Development Company, Jack Taylor was for 20 years Mayacamas' sole wine maker, vineyard manager, viticulturist and chemist.

The Taylors became wine growers for the simple reason that they had always liked fine wines. They decided, in 1941, on the Mt. Veeder property because of its beautiful setting, its excellent grape growing location and because there was a winery and distillery there, dating back to 1889 and known for a time as Mount Veeder Vineyards.

The old vineyards were all ripped out, terraced at great expense, fenced to keep out the deer who are connoisseurs of the better grapes, and replanted mostly to Chardonnay, yielding the wine in which the Taylors specialized with justified pride.

In 1961 the Taylors turned the management of Mayacamas over to younger people, and in 1968 control was acquired by Robert Travers, who is carrying on in the best traditions. An investment banker who apprenticed himself to Joe Heitz in St. Helena to learn the wine trade, Travers has expanded the storage and has added new vineyards of Cabernet Sauvignon and Chardonnay, which are specialties.

For years Mayacamas wines were available only at the winery on an exclusive basis. However, expansion has made it possible for them to be sold through stores and restaurants.

Travers, who is president and winemaker, has earned a justifiably fine reputation since taking over Mayacamas. He discontinued a line called *Lokoya*, which included vermouth, sparkling and inexpensive table wines, and Mayacamas now markets only three exceptionally fine varietals: Chardonnay, Zinfandel and Cabernet Sauvignon (with about 10% Merlot blended in).

Elinor Travers, wife of the winemaker, is secretary of Mayacamas Vineyards, Peter Dahl is business manager, Dwight Price is vineyard manager, Gary Farwell is equipment manager and Jeffery Baker is cellarmaster.

Incidentally, since the question is asked often (and to correct a mistake perpetuated in earlier editions of this book), Travers said, "My latest and best (I think) information is that the local Indian tribe here was called something similar to Mayacamas, and that Lokoya meant elk."

Stag's Leap Wine Cellars, Napa

Named for the rocky escarpment in the nearby hills, this well-designed and beautifully-equipped small winery was completed in time for the 1973 crush on a secluded spot shielded by large oaks from the Silverado Trail. Nearby is the 40-acre Stag's Leap vineyard, which was planted to Cabernet Sauvignon with some Merlot in 1970.

The enterprise was started by Warren Winiarski, a former teacher of political theory at the University of Chicago, and his wife, Barbara, who moved to California in 1964 to find a place in the wine business. With wide experience including stints at Souverain and Robert Mondavi Winery, Winiarski carefully selected the site for the vineyards about six miles north of Napa. A second partnership was formed, and construction of the winery started in 1972.

By the end of 1974, three vintage-dated wines had been released, Cabernet Sauvignon and two Johannisberg Rieslings crushed separately from different vineyards. The Cabernet was made exclusively of grapes from the home vineyard and finished in small French oak barrels. The two whites, one from Birkmyer Vineyards in Wild Horse Valley overlooking San Pablo Bay and the other from Mendocino County grapes, were aged in tanks of Yugoslavian oak. All were wines of unusual quality and were well-received by those lucky enough to taste them. Production will increase gradually to a planned level of about 15,000 cases a year, which should allow fairly wide distribution.

The Winiarskis and their children live in a sprawling 60-year-old ranch house overlooking the Silverado Trail and commanding a magnificent view of the outcropping from which the winery takes its name. Since the stony ridge has long been a geographical landmark in the Napa Valley, at least one other winery has used the name, but it should not be confused with Stag's Leap Wine Cellars.

Veedercrest Vineyards, Napa

Grapes were first planted on the land that is now Veedercrest Vineyards in the 1860s, but the old winery on the property was abandoned during Prohibition and the vineyards fell to decay during World War II. After the Veedercrest partnership was formed in 1972, the owners began planting about 100 acres in the Mayacamas Mountains northwest of Napa to prime varietals. The same year

A. W. Baxter, a management consultant, former hobby winemaker and one of the firm's two general partners, began making wine at a pilot-scale winery with the best urban view of any winery in the country—his home in the Oakland hills overlooking San Francisco Bay.

As the vineyards mature, the winery operations were to be moved to the Napa Valley and production of about 20,000 cases a year was expected to be reached by 1980.

The wines made by Baxter from purchased grapes during the early years of the winery were Merlot (with a Cabernet Sauvignon blend), Cabernet Sauvignon, Pinot Noir, Petite Sirah Rosé, Chardonnay and White Riesling (both late-picked spatlese, and a beerenauslese from selected raisined grapes). All were identified by vineyard on the labels. Eventually, Veedercrest will specialize in Chardonnay, White Riesling, Merlot and Cabernet Sauvignon from its own vineyards, with some blending of other red Bordeaux types in the latter two.

The first wines won a number of awards, and by early 1975 were marketed on a limited basis nationwide.

SOLANO COUNTY

Cadenasso Wine Company, Fairfield

Here at Fairfield, Solano County, in the Suisun district is to be found the Cadenasso Winery, producer of some fine table wines, including Grey Riesling, Grignolino, Pinot Noir and Zinfandel. It is a family owned enterprise now operated by Frank Cadenasso, his wife Joan and their four children. The featured brands are *Cadenasso* and *Solano Vineyards*.

The Cadenasso Wine Company was founded in 1906 when Giovanni Cadenasso, who had immigrated from Italy shortly before, started his own vineyard and winery on the Rutherford Ranch in Green Valley, north of Cordelia. In 1916 Giovanni moved to Fairfield and planted vineyards on the site where the Solano County

Hospital now stands. With Prohibition, wine making came to an end and the winery was dismantled and Giovanni sold his property to the County. Wine making, however, remained in his blood. So undaunted, he started a third vineyard in 1926, aided by his son Frank, across the road from his former location. This he did in the firm conviction that Prohibition would be repealed. He had judged rightly and when Repeal came his vineyards were prospering once more.

Giovanni Cadenasso has now passed on and so Frank is now the owner, winemaker and vineyard manager, assisted, as stated above, by his family. His uncle Giuseppe Cadenasso, Giovanni's brother, was the well known painter who taught art at Mills College.

C. *ALAMEDA—CONTRA COSTA DISTRICT*

This district, as famous in its own way as that of Napa-Solano, consists of a number of separate wine producing areas.

Celebrated throughout the country and beyond is Alameda County's Livermore Valley, home of unsurpassed California wines of the Sauterne types. Some red table wine is also produced as are sparkling wines and aperitif or dessert wines of great merit. The Livermore Valley, actually not so much a valley as a wide basin, comprises two neighboring wine growing areas, the famed vineyards centering around the town of Livermore, with their gravelly vineyards, and separated from them only by some low hills to the west, the sector around Pleasanton.

Second only in importance to the Livermore Valley is southern Alameda with its wine growing center of Mission San Jose.

The rural areas of both counties have continued to shrink before the onslaught of the bulldozer, although some vintners have held on tenaciously in the face of urban sprawl, smog and higher property taxes. Very little vineyard land remains in Contra Costa County, once famous for the vines that grew in the shadow of 4,000-foot Mt.

Diablo. In Walnut Creek subdivisions crowd the ranch where the legendary Jim Howe, retired newspaper and wire service correspondent, had his experimental Gopher Gulch Wine Cellars. At what is now a freeway interchange in Castro Valley, Paul Rhodes, a fifth-generation German winemaker, had followed his craft for nearly 30 years after Prohibition.

Still, there seems to be room in the area for the small as well as the large winery. At Martinez the J. E. Digardi winery is still operated by the grandson of the man who founded it in 1886. In 1965 Davis Bynum founded his winery in downtown Albany, gradually prospered and finally moved to the Russian River Valley. And as late as 1971, R. B. Sanders, D. L. Viale and B. F. Mason established a new enterprise, Chateau Vintners, in San Leandro.

ALAMEDA COUNTY—THE LIVERMORE VALLEY

Concannon Vineyard, Livermore

An old firm with a famous name, well known for its premium wines. The main accent is on the production of white table wines as is to be expected in the heart of the Livermore Valley district.

James Concannon, the founder, was born in the Aran Islands, County Galway, Ireland in 1847 and as a youth determined to carve out a career for himself in what he called "that shining land across the seas."

He saved up enough money for his passage and after holding various jobs in the East could afford to be married by 1874 and a year later brought his bride to San Francisco.

In the West James Concannon found full opportunity to apply his energy and resourcefulness. He pioneered the rubber stamp business on the Pacific Coast and included Mexico in his travels. In Mexico City he criticized the then prevailing sanitary conditions in no uncertain terms with the result that the famed dictator of Mexico, Porfirio Diaz, sent for him. Diaz took a liking to the forthright and energetic young man and entrusted him with full authority to remedy the situation.

The rubber printing stamp, however, was what made Concannon's fortune. By 1883 he had amassed sufficient capital to settle down with his family and farm. It was at the advice of his friend, the colorful Archbishop of San Francisco, Joseph S. Alemany, that James Concannon decided to produce wines for religious use and that he purchased, in the Livermore Valley, a suitable ranch from Horace Overacher, a homesteader. Concannon's success as a vineyardist and winemaker became rapidly established and the high traditions he set have been carried on down continuously to this day.

After James Concannon died in 1911, operation of the winery was continued by his five sons; James, John, Robert, Thomas and Joseph. During Prohibition, while only Sacramental wine was produced, management fell to "Captain Joe" Concannon (so named because of his service as a Cavalry officer during the 1916–1918 expedition against Pancho Villa in Mexico). Eventually, "Captain Joe" and his wife acquired full ownership and he remained as president until his death in 1965. His widow still lives on the ranch, which has been expanded to include more than 300 acres. The other four brothers have since passed away.

The third generation of Concannons now operates the winery, with Joseph Jr. as president and James as vice president, winemaker and chemist. Shares in the corporation remain with members of the immediate family.

Concannon Vineyard has undergone an extensive replanting program in the past decade, with future plans placing emphasis on Johannisberg Riesling in the whites and Petite Sirah and Cabernet Sauvignon in the reds. Champagnes, for sale only at the winery, were added to the line in 1958 to commemorate the 75th year of the firm.

As in the case of the Wente family across the road, the Concannons have felt the pressure of urbanization. For some years they have been farming a portion of the former Hallcrest Vineyards in the Santa Cruz Mountains overlooking the San Lorenzo Valley, first planted to Cabernet Sauvignon and Johannisberg Riesling by the late attorney and enophile Chaffee Hall in 1941.

Joe and Jim Concannon have always had a reputation for adventurous innovation. In the fall of 1974, for instance, they released a very limited quantity of Rkatsiteli, the first wine made in the United States from that Soviet white wine grape of the Caucasus.

Concannon Vineyard is the brand featured and the following table wines are marketed:

WHITE: Sauvignon Blanc, Johannisberg Riesling, Dry Sauterne (dry Semillon), Chateau Concannon (sweet Semillon), Chablis, Moselle, White Dinner Wine;

RED: Petite Sirah (the first bottled in California), Cabernet Sauvignon (limited bottling, Vintage), Red Dinner Wine, Burgundy;

ROSÉ: Vin Rosé (slightly sweet) and Zinfandel Rosé (exceedingly dry).

Aperitif and dessert wines are also marketed including a Vintage Muscat de Frontignan (18% alcohol), an exceptional sweet dessert wine with a pronounced but delicate perfume and flavor, and *Prelude* Dry Sherry, one of the best of the "new" 17% Sherries.

The *Concannon* Champagnes (see also above) are bottle fermented and produced from the Concannon Livermore Vineyards. They include a *Brut,* one of Californias driest with a sugar content of less than 1% and an *Extra Dry,* in the medium range of dryness.

Wente Bros., Livermore

Bearing one of the greatest names in the California wine industry, the Wente family produces some of the finest white table wines of the country, notably of the sauterne and white burgundy varieties.

Carl H. Wente, the founder of the firm, was a native of Hanover, Germany, and came to this country in 1880. He received his first experience in California wine making under the personal supervision of Charles Krug, the great pioneer viticulturist of Napa Valley. Carl Wente soon branched out for himself and purchased, late in the fall of 1883, some vineyards in the Livermore Valley south of the town of Livermore. On this land the original Wente winery still stands.

From the beginning Carl Wente specialized in the production of the finest quality table wines, for which he found a ready market and at prices considerably higher than the average at that time. Both the Semillon and Sauvignon blanc grapes of the Sauternes region in France soon proved themselves to be particularly well suited to the Livermore soil and climate, and so, later on, did the Chardonnay of white burgundy and champagne fame.

Gradually the Wente holdings were extended, first by the founder and later on by his sons, Ernest and Herman Wente. An important acquisition was that of the neighboring El Mocho vineyards. When that highly regarded wine growing pioneer of the Livermore Valley, Louis Mel, retired at an advanced age, he sold his treasured El Mocho property to the Wentes. Mrs. Mel-de-Bire was a friend of the contemporary Marquis de Lur-Saluces, owner of the world renowned Château d'Yquem in Sauternes, near Bordeaux in France, and when Charles Wetmore, as delegate of the California Vinicultural Society and the founder of Cresta Blanca, was charged with obtaining cuttings of the finest European vine varieties, she gave him a letter of introduction to the proprietor of Yquem. Wetmore returned with cuttings of the Semillon, Sauvignon blanc, and Muscadelle du Bordelais vines from the vineyards of Château d'Yquem itself and naturally gave some to Louis Mel, who propagated them in his El Mocho vineyards. When the present Marquis de Lur-Saluces visits California, he never fails to call on the Wentes to enquire how his "California Yquem children" are faring and to taste with appreciation what California is capable of producing in the way of sauternes.

Karl L. Wente, grandson of the founder, is now president and general manager of the Wente operation. He is fortunate in having the wise counsel of his father, Ernest, who remains the farmer and wine grower, and in having the promise of continuity in his two sons, Eric and Philip. Herman Wente—unassuming and simple but regarded by many as the greatest winemaker in California—died in 1961.

Much of the soil of the Wente vineyards is alluvial deposit, washed down from the hills to the east and containing considerable heavy gravel, well suited to the finer grape varieties that like to mature the hard way. The sight of these gravelly vineyards is a perpetual source of wonderment to the novice.

The grapes are picked, variety by variety, at the peak of ripeness for wine making.

The Wentes are optimistic as to the future and are planting more vineyards to the fine varieties so suited to the Livermore area. The winery, too, has been modernized with a new building, new bottling equipment and air-conditioning for the best protection of their wines.

Under pressure from residential development in the Livermore Valley, the Wentes explored and tested other California soils and climates until they found what they believe is an ideal location for new vineyards in Arroyo Seco Canyon at the end of Carmel Valley Road 15 miles from the Pacific in Monterey County. There, in rocky soil warmed by day and cooled by valley breezes at night, they have planted varieties such as Pinot noir, Gamay, Pinot blanc, Chenin blanc and White and Grey Riesling.

The famous specialties of the Wentes are their white table wines, unsurpassed in California.

Most of the varietals carry the vintage date. *Only* table wines are produced, all marketed under the *Wente Bros.* brand. Two standard wines are marketed, a red and a white under the *Valle de Oro* label, the romantic name which the Spaniards gave to the Livermore Valley.

The following *Wente Bros.* wines are available:

In the Sauterne style bottle: Dry Semillon and Sauvignon Blanc. Chateau Wente, produced from a blend of Semillon and Sauvignon blanc with the addition of a little Muscadelle du Bordelais and as fine a sweet wine of the Sauterne order as can be produced in California is only available in the Western part of the United States as the amount of the wine is limited.

In the Rhine wine style bottle: Grey Riesling.

In the Burgundy style bottle: Pinot Chardonnay, Pinot Blanc and Chablis. A new addition has been *Le Blanc de Blancs,* a blend of Chenin blanc and Ugni blanc grapes.

Although the Wente winery is best known for its white table wines it also produces Petite Sirah, Gamay Beaujolais, Pinot Noir and a very popular Rosé made predominantly from the Gamay and Grenache grapes.

Villa Armando Winery, Pleasanton

This operation passed into its present ownership in 1962 when the old Garatti holdings at Pleasanton were purchased by Anthony D. Scotto of New York, a member of a family which has grown and made wines for more than a century in Italy and the United States.

The original winery was founded in 1902 by Frank Garatti, a native of the Italian province of Lombardy. He planted the vineyards and ran the company until his death in 1948. His son-in-law, F. W. Brenner, took over until he, too, died in 1960. Under the Villa Armando Winery ownership Robert F. Diana, well known in California wine circles, became general manager.

Most Villa Armando wines are shipped to the Metropolitan New York area, but an increasing amount is sold in California stores and through a retail outlet at the winery. A new tasting room and expanded wine touring facilities were completed.

Several generics are available under the *Villa Armando* brand, including Chablis, Sauterne, Burgundy, Chianti, Rubinello, Orobianco and Vino Rustico. Varietals offered are Barbera, Pinot Noir, Zinfandel, Malvasia Bianca and Semillon.

SOUTHERN ALAMEDA COUNTY
(Mission San Jose District)

Llords & Elwood Winery, Mission San Jose

A tragedy befell California's wine industry when, on October 25, 1974, Mike Elwood died unexpectedly of a heart attack just short of his 70th birthday.

Most wineries are founded by winemakers who, because of the necessities of commerce, eventually become salesmen of at least their own brands. With the growing firm of Llords & Elwood the situation was reversed. By the time J. H. (Mike) Elwood decided to become a winemaker, he already had devoted nearly 20 years to becoming one of Southern California's best known retailers of high quality wines and spirits.

A native Californian, Elwood left the outdoor advertising business with Repeal and opened a small package store in the Los Angeles area. The company expanded, catering to customers who knew and appreciated fine wines and spirits, and by the time he and his attractive wife, Irene, sold it in 1961 to devote their full attention to the Llords & Elwood Winery, the chain consisted of stores in West Hollywood, Beverly Hills and Brentwood. They kept the firm's name (Llords had been added when Elwood acquired a store by that name), and today it is associated with one of California's leading lines of premium wines.

The Elwoods had traveled widely, and their knowledge of the finest wines of Europe reveals itself in their products.

The Llords & Elwood Winery was started with the cooperation and encouragement of Rudolf Weibel of Weibel Champagne Vineyards (see there). In 1955 the Elwoods built their winery adjacent to the Weibel facilities in Fremont's Mission San Jose District about 40 miles southeast of San Francisco. The first wines produced were two Sherries and a Port which entered the retail market in the fall of 1961. Since that time seven other wines have been added—five table varietals, an excellent bulk fermented Champagne and another Sherry. A bottle-fermented Champagne replaced the original in 1972.

Although the future of the winery is not in doubt, and it will continue to expand and make wines of the quality that earned it an international reputation, it will miss the personal stamp of Mike Elwood, who was his own grape buyer and winemaker. An earlier blow to the family company was the death of winery superintendent Sal Vacari, a long-time associate who oversaw the operations at Mission San Jose and at the cellars and other facilities at San Jose, Livermore and Fresno.

The Elwoods' son, Richard, headquartered in Beverly Hills, remains president of the firm, a position he has held since 1969. Mrs. Elwood is vice president of the company, and Richard's wife, Mary, is secretary.

Llords & Elwood wines are now sold in leading retail outlets and can be found in fine restaurants. An interesting feature of the line is the use of proprietary names for varietal wines. For instance, their Johannisberg Riesling carries the name "Castle Magic" and the Pinot Noir is called "Velvet Hill."

The other wines:

RED: Cabernet Sauvignon;

WHITE: The Rare Chardonnay;

ROSÉ: Rosé of Cabernet (made with Cabernet Sauvignon grapes);

SHERRY: Great Day D-r-ry Sherry, Dry Wit Sherry, The Judge's Secret Cream Sherry;

PORT: Ancient Proverb Port.

Weibel Champagne Vineyards (Weibel, Inc.), Mission San Jose

Weibel Champagne Vineyards, founded in 1939, produces champagnes, table and aperitif and dessert wines which have established an excellent reputation for themselves. It is a family enterprise, owned and operated by Frederick E. Weibel, president and general manager. Fred Weibel Jr. is executive vice president.

The Weibels are natives of Münsingen, Canton of Bern, Switzerland. The late Rudolf Weibel had been engaged in the wine and champagne business in his native country and in France and came to the United States as an importer of wines and brandies in 1934. He traveled all over the country and, when he came to California, observed its climate and soil, the fine wine grapes which could be grown and the quality of wines it was possible to produce. Comparing them type by type with those of Europe, he made up his mind to emigrate to the United States and devote himself in California to the production of the finest wines that could be made. So he came to this country in 1936 for good, accompanied by his son Frederick.

The Weibels first settled in San Francisco making champagne from purchased wines while looking around for a suitable winery and vineyard property. This they found in their ranch and winery near Mission San Jose* on the Warm Springs site of the old Leland Stanford Winery. Late in September 1958 the State Historical Landmarks Advisory Committee held formal dedication ceremonies on the Weibel property, erecting a landmark inscribed "Leland Stanford Winery—Founded 1869" in the presence of some 500 officials and other guests.

The site was famous long before the coming of the Spanish Conquistadores. Indians used to frequent the warm springs to benefit by their healing capacities. It was a dedicated area and no tribal wars were fought in the vicinity.

A Spanish land grant gave a vast territory, including the Mission, to the Higuera family in 1836 who named it "Rancho del Agua Caliente" on account of its warm springs. In 1860 Clement Colombet bought a large acreage of the Rancho upon which he built a fashionable resort, the Warm Springs Hotel, surrounded by vineyards. The Hotel flourished until it was wrecked by the earthquake of 1868.

The following year Leland Stanford, railroad builder, Governor, Senator, and founder of Stanford University, bought a square mile of land at Warm Springs. His brother, Josiah, planted some 350 acres of

* Founded by Father Junipero Serra in 1797.

vines there and built a winery with a capacity of some 500,000 gallons, later adding a brandy distillery. Warm Springs did a flourishing business, large quantities of "Stanford" wine being sold. Leland Stanford deeded the property to his brother Josiah, and encouraged by the latter's success in the wine business and affirming his belief that California was the world's best wine country he embarked on his famous wine growing project at Vina, Tehama County, an enterprise which lasted well into the twentieth century. The Weibels purchased their ranch in 1945 and devoted the next few years to replanting the vineyards and modernizing the winery. They have steadily been expanding their business capturing also the Eastern markets.

After nearly 30 years at Mission San Jose, the Weibels have opened a second winery in Redwood Valley just north of Ukiah in Mendocino County. Attached is a tasting room with a dramatic laminated-beam roof made in the shape of an inverted champagne glass, said to be the biggest wine tasting room in America.

Weibel is the featured brand for all products sold directly to the public.

The bottle fermented *Weibel* Champagnes include Chardonnay *Brut, Brut, Extra Dry, Sec,* Pink Champagne and Sparkling Burgundy. Other Sparkling Wines produced are their Crackling Rosé and Moscato Spumante (Sparkling Muscat) and a trademarked specialty, Crackling Duck.

Both generic and varietal table wines are available, the latter including:

WHITE: Chardonnay, Johannisberg Riesling, Chenin Blanc, Green Hungarian and Grey Riesling;

RED: Pinot Noir, Cabernet Sauvignon, Royalty, Gamay Beaujolais and Zinfandel;

ROSÉ: Grenache Rosé.

Estate Bottled Vintage Chardonnay and Pinot Noir are available in limited quantities.

Aperitif and dessert wines, including Dry and Sweet Vermouth, are produced and include "Dry Bin" Cocktail Flor Sherry (dry), "Gallery" Flor Sherry (medium), "Amberina" Cream Flor Sherry (sweet), "Governor's Rare" Solera Port and "Memento" Cream of Black Muscat.

The *Weibel* Brandy is a fairly recent addition but not so the wine called "Tangor" with a flavor of tangerines, the winery claiming to be the originator of the "Natural Flavored Wines" (see Chapter VIII).

CONTRA COSTA COUNTY

Conrad Viano Winery, Martinez

The Viano family vineyards have been nestled in a small valley almost within sight of Suisun Bay since Prohibition. Theirs is the only significant vineyard land left in Contra Costa County, in an area once so rich in grapes it was called Vine Hill. Despite the tremendous pressure of residential development and the high taxation which accompanies it, the Vianos have steadfastly resisted the bulldozer and are, in fact, replanting to expensive varietals.

The vineyards were established by the late Clement Viano, scion of a centuries-old winemaking family from Italy's Piedmont region. In 1946 the present winery was established by Conrad Viano, and it has been expanded several times since. At the present time there are three generations involved in the business including the four children of young Clement Viano, the grandson of the founder and a 1958 graduate in viticulture of the University of California at Davis. Clement operates the winery with his father, Conrad (from whom it gets its name), his mother Carmen, and his wife, Sharon.

Clement Viano is an enthusiastic and tireless winemaker who has modernized the plant and, in keeping with the motto he dreamed up ("It's the Grapes"), experiments with both red and white varietals.

Viano is the brand for bulk Zinfandel, Burgundy, Sauterne and Vin Rosé. The *Viano Private Stock* label is reserved for the following premium generics and varietals:

RED: Barbera, Burgundy, Cabernet Sauvignon, Gamay, Zinfandel;
WHITE: Chablis, Grey Riesling;
ROSÉ: Grenache Rosé and Zinfandel Rosé.

In addition Sherry, Port and Muscatel are available. *Viano Reserve Selection* is the label for limited bottlings of vintage wines.

D. *SANTA CLARA—SANTA CRUZ AND SAN BENITO DISTRICT*

The neighboring counties of Santa Clara and Santa Cruz, with the Santa Cruz Mountains forming the border between the two, are usually grouped together as one wine growing district. Extensions of this district include the wine growing areas in San Benito County and in San Luis Obispo County.

Santa Clara County can be divided into three wine growing areas, spreading west and east from the Santa Clara Valley floor to the adjoining hills and mountains.

West of the Santa Clara Valley, in the foothills, lies Los Gatos, and higher yet, in the hills beyond, Saratoga, together forming the Los Gatos-Saratoga area. Here are the homes of some of the finest table wines and champagnes of California, while fine aperitif or dessert wines are also produced.

To the east of San Jose lies the hillside Evergreen area with its vineyards stretching onto the slopes of Mt. Hamilton. From this section hail a number of superior table wines.

The southern part of Santa Clara County and of its valley is noted for an important winery section, centering around Morgan Hill, San Martin and Gilroy, with good wines of all types being produced from the neighboring hillsides. Many a sound "country" table wine also is produced in the small wineries, run mostly by Americans of Italian descent, in the section west of Gilroy up towards the Hecker Pass and in the Uvas area.

Santa Cruz County is equally noteworthy for its wines. Some excellent table wines are produced above Felton and at Soquel. Besides there are scattered vineyard areas in the county including Vinehill, towards Los Gatos, Bonny Doon, southwest of Ben Lomond, Boulder Creek, north of that Scottish-named elevation, and Laurel area in the mountains towards the Santa Clara County line, and the Casserly section, up towards Mt. Madonna.

Once again the pressure of urban expansion has pushed the vineyards away from the cities. The growth of San Jose and related suburbs has given rise to the planting of vast new vineyard tracts to the south in San Benito and Monterey Counties.

And again, new wineries are joining older, small family operations. In 1971 Thomas Kruse bonded his namesake winery at Gilroy. In 1972 Mario and Frances Fortino established the Hecker Winery near Gilroy and began making a variety of good wines, some estate bottled. Mario had more than two decades of experience, some in Italy. The nearby Fortino Winery at Gilroy has been in business since 1948. In 1973 Nathaniel and Jan Sherrill founded Sherrill Cellars at Woodside on the San Francisco Peninsula. And in 1970 near Hollister Drive, Rodney W. Ballard, an enologist who received his Ph.D. in microbiology from the University of California, started one of the state's most interesting new wineries, San Benito Vineyards, which specializes exclusively in premium fruit and berry wines.

Peter Scagliotti's Live Oaks Winery and the Anselmo Conrotto Winery, both at Gilroy, date back to 1912 and 1933 respectively. The latter year, just after Repeal, also saw the beginning of the Emilio Guglielmo Winery at Morgan Hill, a proud family enterprise that produces the well-known Mt. Madonna varietals.

Santa Clara Valley—Los Gatos, Saratoga District

Almadén Vineyards, Los Gatos

About midway between Los Gatos and the former quicksilver mining village of New Almadén* and some five miles south of San Jose are to be found the winery and domain of Almadén, overlooking the undulating hills towards Loma Prieta and the Mountains that separate Santa Clara and Santa Cruz Counties. Here some of the finest California champagnes are produced as well as table and aperitif and dessert wines of great merit.

The founder of Almadén was Etienne Thée, a farmer from Bordeaux in France who is said to have been lured to California by the Gold Rush. In any case he devoted himself to less elusive and more permanent pursuits, grape growing and wine making. To this end he purchased from the Guadalajara pioneer José Augustin Narvaez part of the old Rancho San Juan Bautista, securing for himself a fertile tract of land along the creek called Guadalupe River. Here in 1847 he built his home, that still stands today, on a high knoll with its sweeping view of the valley and of the mountains beyond.

Thée was soon joined in his enterprise by a neighbor and compatriot, Charles Lefranc, said to have been a tailor in Passy, the suburb of Paris. The vineyards were planted in 1852 cuttings of choice vines imported from the districts of Champagne, Bordeaux, Burgundy and the Rhône Valley. Lefranc married Thée's daughter, Adèle, and eventually inherited his father-in-law's property. He prospered together with his vineyards and by the end of the eighteen seventies could boast that they contained more vines than any other in the county and, what was more important, that his wines rated with the best. The finest cooperage was imported from France around Cape Horn, some of it in use down to the present. Many were the famous

---

* So named by the Spaniards after the quicksilver mines of Almadén in the Province of Ciudad Real, New Castile, Spain.

guests who enjoyed Lefranc's hospitality, among whom are said to have been numbered Admiral Farragut and Generals Sherman, Halleck and Ulysses S. Grant.

The French influence and atmosphere were dominant at Almadén and this tradition was strengthened when Lefranc hired a young Burgundian to help in the office and winery. This was Paul Masson who was to make his own name great in the California wine industry and followed precedent by marrying Lefranc's daughter, Louise. Eventually Masson became associated with his father-in-law in the production and merchandising of champagnes and table wines in a jointly owned business, Lefranc-Masson. Later he established himself on his own property in the hills above Saratoga (see Paul Masson Vineyards).

Almadén (the property was given the district name of Almadén in 1941) was inherited by Charles Lefranc's son Henry and after the latter's death in 1909 was held in trust for the family until it was sold to Charles Jones. With the advent of Prohibition Almadén entered a dormant period as far as wine making is concerned.

In 1941 Louis A. Benoist, well known San Francisco businessman and president of the Lawrence Warehouse Company, national field warehousing concern, purchased the property at the advice of the noted wine authority Frank Schoonmaker. Oliver J. Goulet, one of the foremost experts in the field, was engaged as winemaker and plant manager. In this capacity he was ably assisted after 1954 by A. C. (Al) Huntsinger, now winemaker for Geyser Peak Winery in Sonoma County.

The winery and other buildings were renovated and the original vineyards were brought into shape. Additional acreage was acquired, planted to the finest varietals.

In 1967 Almadén was taken over by National Distillers which operates it as a subsidiary. German-trained Klaus Mathes is now winemaker.

Recent winery expansions include a new champagne cellar and a sherry room featuring six Soleras, making Almadén's Solera operation one of the most modern and largest in the country. A huge binning cellar for bottle aging red table wines houses inventories of Cabernet Sauvignon and Pinot Noir with the purpose of aging red wines at least two years in glass before placing them on the market.

Almadén's acreage was increased in 1955 by the purchase of the Sykes Ranch at Paicines near Hollister in San Benito County in the area of the Pinnacles where the legendary bandit Joaquin Murietta hid out during his brief and bloody career. The rolling hills on which cattle grazed have been transformed into extended mountain vineyards to assure adequate supply and reserve of choice wine variety grapes to meet the steadily increasing demand for the finer varietal wines. Here also, at Paicines, a crushing operation and a distillery, for brandy production, are located.

San Benito County, in the area around Hollister, has for long had an enviable reputation for yielding premium wines. Its best known wine enterprise, Valliant Vineyards, is now also operated by Almadén. The Paicines and Valliant Vineyards, total more than 4,300 acres.

Today, white wines are made at Paicines where Almadén, reputedly the first winery to bring them from Germany, has a battery of Willmes presses. Wines are giving their initial aging and then are shipped to Los Gatos for further aging and bottling. Red wines and Ports are produced at the Cienega winery located along the foothills of a parallel valley to Paicines. Built in the 1880's by Hollister mayor William Palmtag, the winery stands astride the San Andreas Fault and has attracted seismologists from all over the world to see the cleft in the floor kept open by earth tremors. Cienega houses the largest cellars in the world for table wines and Sherries, with more than 65,000 small oak barrels in its interior.

Another important vineyard belonging to Almadén is located at Pleasanton in the celebrated Livermore Valley white table wine district.

The change of Almadén from a small producer of premium wines to one of the giants in the industry has been dramatic. Sales grew from about 73,000 cases in 1952 to nearly 6,000,000 in the mid-1970s. From one winery with a few hundred acres of vineyard, the company has expanded to a complex of four wineries with a combined capacity of more than 24,000,000 gallons and a total of nearly 7,000 acres of vineyards. When the new vineyards at King City and San Lucas in Monterey County began producing in 1973, it brought the total number of vines under Almadén control to almost 3,500,000. In 1972 a new distribution center at San Jose raised the corporation's bottle-aging capacity by 1,250,000 cases, and a winery acquired at Kingsburg near Fresno late in 1973 added 6,000,000 gallons of bulk storage.

Almadén Vineyards produces a complete selection of wines marketing them under the *Almadén* label.

The sparkling wines (bottle fermented) number the *Blanc de Blancs,* made from Chardonnay, *Brut, Extra Dry* (medium) as well as Rosé (Pink) Champagne and the inevitable Sparkling Burgundy. Le Domaine is the brand of cheaper sparkling wines.

Table wines include generic types such as the Mountain Reds and Whites and Estate-Bottled Vintage varietals as well of course as the varietals.

The three *Almadén* Sherries are of the *flor* type and blended and aged according to the Solera system: Solera Cocktail (dry), Solera Golden (medium) and Solera Cream (sweet). The Solera Ruby and Tawny Ports are also blended and aged in the same manner. *Almadén* Vermouth comes in Pale Triple Dry and Sweet types. In 1952 the winery launched its "Centennial Brandy" to celebrate the 100th year of its establishment.

In June of 1974 Almadén took back from National Distillers, which had it as a separate label, the sale and distribution of *Almadén* Brandy. It will be produced in the Kingsburg winery in the San Joaquin Valley.

David Bruce, Los Gatos

A San Jose physician who spent eight years studying wine making and vineyard techniques before taking the plunge, David Bruce purchased his vineyard property high in the mountains above Los Gatos in 1961. Assisted by his family he planted nearly 25 acres of Chardonnay, White Riesling, Cabernet Sauvignon and Pinot Noir. Although the original winery wasn't built until 1964, it rapidly was outgrown and construction of a new 6,000 square foot concrete building was completed in 1968. An innovator who designs much of his own equipment, Bruce plans some new processing techniques when the new winery is in operation.

To help meet the growing demand for his wines, Bruce purchased another 15 acres in the Santa Cruz Mountains, and other future vineyard acquisitions are planned. Although *David Bruce* wines have been available primarily from the winery, they will appear in selected retail outlets. Offered (all Vintage and 100% varietal) are Chardonnay, Pinot Noir, Cabernet Sauvignon and Zinfandel. White Riesling, Grenache and Petite Sirah have been added.

Novitiate Wines, Los Gatos

In the hills above Los Gatos one finds the magnificently situated Novitiate Winery.

Since its founding in 1888 the Novitiate has maintained the tradition for producing fine altar wines in strict accordance with the Canon Law of the Roman Catholic Church. Once the needs for sacramental wines is met, the remainder of the production is made available to the public through commercial channels.

The Jesuit Fathers and Brothers have full charge of the production of the wines. The novices and junior students help pick most of the grapes each fall. Many of the vines were imported from France, as were the muscats from the Montpellier region near the Mediterranean.

Father Francis J. Silva, S.J., is the president of the Novitiate, while Father Henri Charvet, S.J., is vice president and vineyard manager; Father Louis B. Franklin, S.J. is vice president and general manager; Brother Lee Williams, S.J., is the winemaker and Father James E. Ransford is the chemist.

The Novitiate's Altar Wines are only available to the clergy. They are similar or identical to the wines marketed for the public (see below) but are in each case labeled with a distinctive name, appropriate to the particular wine.

A listing of the Novitiate's Altar Wines follows:

"Manresa" (Red Burgundy), "Villa Joseph" (Sauterne), "Vin Doré" (Sweet Sauterne), "San Carlos" (Chablis), "Santa Rosa" (Grenache Rosé);

"Villa Maria" (medium dry sherry), "San Pedro" (Port), "San Ignacio" (Tokay), "L'Admirable" (Angelica), "Guadalupe" (Muscat de Frontignan), "San Jose" (Red Muscat).

Available to the public under the *Novitiate* brand are the following table and aperitif and dessert wines, all in the premium class:

Table wines: Burgundy, Sauterne and Chablis in the generics and Cabernet Sauvignon, Pinot Noir, Zinfandel, Pinot Blanc, Chenin Blanc and Grenache Rosé in the varietals.

Dry Semillon and Sauvignon Blanc were formerly produced separately but these are now used for reasons of economy in the Dry Sauterne and Chateau Novitiate production, the latter a sweet wine of the Sauterne type. White Riesling is offered when the vintage warrants. A new wine is Dry Malvasia.

The Novitiate is also well known throughout the country for its aperitif and dessert wines. These include Sherry, Dry Sherry, *Flor* Sherry, Cocktail Sherry, Port, Angelica, a wonderful Muscat Frontignan and an altogether exceptional dessert wine (used by many as a cordial), the Black Muscat, made entirely from blended vintages of Muscat Hamburg grapes.

Paul Masson Vineyards, Saratoga

A great name in the history of the California wine industry and a national enterprise, started by that famed Frenchman from Burgundy, Paul Masson, the origin of the enterprise dating back to 1852.

Paul Masson came to work for Charles Lefranc at his winery between Los Gatos and New Almadén, eventually marrying his boss's daughter, Louise (see Almadén Vineyards). He became associated with his father-in-law, the firm being called Lefranc-Masson. After Lefranc's death it bore the name of Paul Masson alone.

In the 1880's Paul Masson established himself on a property in the Santa Cruz Mountains above Saratoga where the soil and climate were eminently suited to the growing of the finer wine grape varieties and planted his vineyards to cuttings to the choicest imported vines. The winery Paul Masson built on this mountain property was partly destroyed by the 1906 earthquake but was rebuilt by him in the following years using some of the sandstone from the old St. Joseph's Church in San Jose which had been destroyed in the same disaster. He also obtained from the ruins of the Church a 12th century Romanesque portal which had originally come from Spain.

Paul Masson made his name forever famous by producing champagnes and table wines of the highest quality. For over half a century he worked in his steeply sloping mountain vineyards and in his wine cellars establishing a great name for his wines and becoming somewhat of a legendary figure himself. For several years he was a Viticultural Commissioner for the State of California. He made frequent trips to his native France, purchasing additional vine cuttings and the latest in winery equipment. One of the firm's earliest awards for fine wines was made at the Paris exhibition of 1900. In 1936 Paul Masson retired from his vineyards and passed away four years later, a greatly respected personality and true modern pioneer of the best that can be produced in California wines.

Before he retired Paul Masson had sold his vineyards and winery to Martin Ray. A disastrous fire occurred in 1941, wrecking the winery and causing great losses but Martin Ray rebuilt both the winery and his business. Two years later he sold the enterprise to Joseph E. Seagram's, the distillers, later establishing another domain of his own even higher up in the mountains. Seagram's operated the Masson winery and vineyards only a short while, being succeeded in 1945 by a company in which Alfred Fromm and the late Franz Sichel were the partners. Both the Fromm and Sichel families have been in the wine industry for a great number of years, the former for five generations and the latter for seven.

Stanford J. Wolf became president in charge of production in 1972. Leo A. Berti, vice president for a number of years, is now semi-retired and works part-time as a quality control specialist for Seagrams wine producing companies throughout the world. He was replaced by Morris Katz as vice president in charge of production, and marketing is handled by Browne Vintners Co., headed by president Arthur L. Palombo.

In 1974 Paul Masson Vineyards broke ground on two large facilities, a $25,000,000 Sherry Cellars surrounded by 500 acres of vineyards eight miles north of Madera, and a new bottle-aging complex in South San Jose that ultimately would cover 1,200,000 square feet and have room for 60,000,000 bottles.

In recent years the Paul Masson firm has extended its vineyard holdings through the purchase of the San Ysidro Ranch near Gilroy which was planted to varietal wines under the supervision of University of California viticultural specialists. In 1962–63, the 1,000-acre Paul Masson Pinnacles Vineyard was planted in Monterey County. Another 500 acres was begun in 1968. Recent plantings will raise the total to 5,000 acres.

In 1959 the firm opened the Paul Masson Champagne Cellars in Saratoga. In view of the historic mountain vineyards the new Champagne Cellars consolidate the bottling, packaging and shipping facilities for the entire Paul Masson line, including the brandy. In a building designed to practice generations old traditions in modern surroundings visitors have the opportunity to observe all wine aging and champagne making operations and to taste the various types of wines produced by Paul Masson. The building is of eye catching modernity with a roof consisting of six huge wood arches. It contains 225,000 square feet and what with the "Champagne" fountain 67 feet high set in a 9,000 square foot reflecting pool and a reception rotunda featuring a spiral ramp to the visitors gallery it is a most impressive sight.

The Saratoga winery is located some three miles to the east of the famous old Paul Masson winery, previously the focal point for visitors. It is here that a natural bowl forms the lovely setting for summer Sunday concerts featuring many a famous artist and it is here on the terrace overlooking the Santa Clara Valley from an imposing height that many an *al fresco* meal has been enjoyed while quaffing some fine Paul Masson table wine or champagne.

Paul Masson Vineyards produces and markets both generic and varietal table wines, sparkling wines, aperitif and dessert wines including vermouth, as well as brandies, all under the *Paul Masson* label.

Proprietary wines include Baroque and Rubion (reds) and Rhine Castle (white).

The regular types of aperitif and dessert wines are marketed both in fifths and in half-gallons while the Rare Dry Sherry, Rare Cream Sherry and Rare Tawny Port come in heart shaped decanters as does the new Rare Souzao Port. The Vermouths include both a Double Dry and a Sweet type.

Paul Masson Vineyards are especially famous for their Sparkling Wines. These include *Brut* Champagne, available also in Magnums and Jeroboams,* Red Champagne (Triple Red), marketed in the same sizes, Extra Dry Champagne, Pink Champagne and Sparkling Burgundy (Cuvée Rouge), all three available in larger bottles also. Another new wine is Crackling Rosé.

---

* Magnums hold 2 bottles while Jeroboams hold twice again as much.

Ridge Vineyards, Cupertino

This is another example of those small California premium wineries which have been started since the war by self-taught winemakers—men following the traditions established by Stewart at Souverain, McCrea at Stony Hill and Zellerbach at Hanzell.

David Bennion, then with the Stanford Research Institute, and three partners purchased a venerable vineyard on the southwest side of Monte Bello Ridge at an altitude of 2,300 feet in 1959. In 1962 they decided to establish a winery. Ridge incorporated in 1967, and Bennion is now president, R. W. Foster is vice president and two of the original partners, H. D. Crane and C. A. Rosen, are secretary and treasurer respectively. Other principal stockholders include Carl Djerassi, Alejandro Zaffaroni and Paul Draper, who replaced Bennion as winemaker in 1970. Draper had made wine in Chile before joining Ridge, and he had studied winemaking in California, Italy and Bordeaux, France.

Much of the property was part of the original Monte Bello Vineyard, and the winery dates back to before the turn of the century. In 1948 William Short acquired the vineyards and began upgrading them, planting Cabernet Sauvignon and Chardonnay. Following the purchase by the present owners additional plantings were undertaken and new property was added, including the original Monte Bello Winery.

All *Ridge Vineyards* wines are vintage-dated and unfiltered. This means the reds, which have a reputation as being among the biggest wines of their type made in America, may throw a deposit in the manner of some of the great wines of Europe. Usually available are estate-grown Chardonnay, estate-grown Cabernet Sauvignon, Petite Sirah, Gamay and a small amount of estate-grown Ruby Cabernet. Ridge is well-known for its Zinfandels, made from grapes harvested from several selected vineyards ranging from Mendocino County to the north all the way to Lodi in the Central Valley.

Gemello Winery, Mountain View

This small family winery, founded in 1934 by John Gemello is situated right off the busy El Camino Real in Mountain View and produces and markets wines for sale mostly in its flourishing retail outlet on Highway 101. John Gemello born near Asti in Piedmont, Italy, the home of some of Italy's most famous wines, retired in 1944 and Mario Gemello, his son, is now president of the enterprise. John Gemello, it may be noted, once worked in the vineyards of and made wine at the original Monte Bello winery now owned by Ridge Vineyards. Little could he have dreamed at that time of the myriads of cars swooshing along El Camino Real in Mountain View and of the enterprise he started, hard to find for those in a hurry but still easy for those who want to locate a small and select winery and retail outlet. In 1969 Louis C. Sarto acquired a one-third interest and took over marketing.

Sarto introduced vintage-dating, back labels, cork identification and the importation of French cooperage to the winery. In July of 1974 the Mike Filice family, formerly of the San Martin Vineyards Co., bought all of the outstanding shares of the Gemello corporation, retaining Gemello as winemaker and Sarto in a marketing capacity.

The Gemello Winery specializes in the finer varietal table wines although the usual types of aperitif and dessert wines are also available, purchased and marketed under the *Gemello's* featured label, *Mountain View* being the secondary brand.

The finer varietal table wines are either purchased or produced at the winery and aged in small oak casks or puncheons and include:

RED: Pinot Noir, Gamay, Zinfandel, Barbera and an especially noteworthy Cabernet Sauvignon made from 100% Cabernet Sauvignon grapes and on the average 8 years old, produced from grapes grown in the Saratoga foothills on land once owned by Paul Masson;

WHITE: Pinot Chardonnay (from grapes grown in the Cote d'Or Mountain area in Santa Clara County), Pinot Blanc (from the

Saratoga district), Sylvaner, Grey Riesling and Riesling (a blend);

ROSÉ: Grenache Rosé, Zinfandel Rosé and Cabernet Rosé.

WOODSIDE-PORTOLA VALLEY

Nepenthe Cellars, Portola Valley

As is the case with Woodside Vineyards and Sherrill Cellars, the only other wineries in San Mateo County, Nepenthe Cellars is just one step removed from the classification of home winery. Bonded in 1967 by George Burtness, a young land management executive at nearby Stanford University, the winery has a permanent staff consisting of Burtness, his wife, Yvonne, and their daughter, Laura.

Originally a hobby winemaker who began experimenting in 1962, Burtness named his venture after the ancient Greek word for a potion to relieve pain and sorrow. Although he tends a small vineyard, most of his grapes are purchased from growers in the Santa Cruz Mountains and upper Napa Valley.

The principal *Nepenthe Cellars* wines are Cabernet Sauvignon and a full aged Zinfandel made in the fashion of Bordeaux. Others include Pinot Noir, Petite Sirah, Chardonnay, White Riesling and a rosé made from Petite Sirah and Pinot Noir.

Woodside Vineyards, Woodside

Robert Lee Mullen was a teetotaler before he came to California in 1955. On the day he arrived he drank his first glass of wine, and he has been a confirmed enophile ever since.

An executive with a national building materials firm, Mullen and his charming wife were living in Woodside when they made their first wine as amateurs in 1960. By the time they obtained their bond in 1963, they had built another home in the same community, this one equipped with a modern and compact winery-laboratory in a specially-built cellar, since expanded. Production now averages 1,500 gallons per year.

In collaboration with close friends, the Robert Groetzingers, the Mullens planted most of their small plot to Chardonnay and Pinot noir. On nearby properties, parts of the original Rixford "La Questa Vineyards" founded in 1883 but long since subdivided, they tend six acres. Now, with assistance from scientists at the University of California in Davis and Oakland wine consultant Julius Fessler (and, of course, the neighbors who help with the harvest), *Woodside Vineyards* is in a position to offer two Vintage whites, Chardonnay and Chenin Blanc, and two Vintage reds, Cabernet Sauvignon and Pinot Noir. The wines, all in the premium class, are sold from the winery and stores in selected cities.

SANTA CLARA VALLEY—SAN JOSE,
EVERGREEN DISTRICT

Mirassou Vineyards, San Jose

The type of operation at Mirassou Vineyards is a unique one, for many years producing varietal table wines and champagne stock of premium quality to be sold in bulk to other wineries. A growing quantity of these wines is bottled and sold to consumers in selected states.

The enterprise is presently operated by Edmund A. and Norbert C. Mirassou, fourth generation wine growers, and their sons, who are continuing the tradition started in Santa Clara Valley by their great-grandfather Pierre Pellier in 1854. It is located in the rolling hills between the Santa Clara Valley and Mount Hamilton in the district known as Evergreen, where they own 350 acres. Another 50 acres is owned at Gilroy, and a new 300-acre vineyard has been founded near Soledad in Monterey County. Another 650 acres has been planted near Soledad by the fifth generation, which also owns and operates the marketing company.

Between 1966, when the company first began to offer its wine under the family label, to 1974, annual sales increased from about 1,000 cases to more than 100,000 cases in 40 states and four countries.

In 1974 the fifth generation of Mirassous acquired the century-old Wehner Winery, most recently operated by the Cribari family in the Mt. Hamilton foothills. The purchase added 500,000 gallons of wood cooperage, increasing the Mirassou wood-aging capacity by over one-third. In spite of the fluctuations in the wine industry in the mid-1970s, the Mirassous had over one million bottles of Au Natural and Brut Champagne and Sparkling Gamay Beaujolais cellared for the 1975 market.

Vintage varietal wines available under the *Mirassou* label include Monterey Riesling (Sylvaner and French Colombard), Johannisberg Riesling, Chenin Blanc, Gewurztraminer, Pinot Chardonnay, Petite Rose (from Petite Sirah and Grenache grapes), Petite Sirah, Gamay Beaujolais, Cabernet Sauvignon and Zinfandel.

Santa Clara Valley—Morgan Hill and Gilroy-Hecker Pass District

Pedrizetti Winery, Morgan Hill

A classic little country winery, Pedrizetti nonetheless produces a few remarkable (and inexpensive) estate-bottled varietals, all 100% of the grape named. The Barbera and Zinfandel are aged five years in wood before bottling.

Edward and Phyllis Pedriezetti took over the winery in 1963 from his father, John. He had purchased it in 1945 from Camillo Colombano, who built it in 1923. The third generation is represented by young Daniel Pedrizetti.

In addition to the two reds mentioned above, the Pedrizettis offer estate-bottled Grenache Rosé and Zinfandel Rosé, as well as whites, aperitif and dessert, sparkling and fruit wines at their tasting room in the "Gallery" just north of Morgan Hill.

Richert & Sons, Inc., Morgan Hill

Walter S. Richert, a 1932 graduate of the University of California, first entered the wine industry in 1937 and has been connected with wineries in various capacities as chemist, winemaker, production manager, sales representative and general manager. He has held important positions in the American Society of Enologists (winemakers) and has been Editor of both *Wine Review* and *Wines and Vines.*

In 1953 he founded his own winery at Morgan Hill on a shoestring, expanding gradually as opportunities permitted. In 1958 he took over the old Paradise Valley Winery at Oak Glenn a few miles west of Morgan Hill.

In 1974 the winery was acquired by Wines Unlimited of Los Angeles, which retained Walter Richert as winemaker and his son, Scott, as general manager. A retail outlet is maintained at the winery, and the four Sherries and two Ports the company continues to specialize in are available through retail outlets.

San Martin Vineyards Company, San Martin

In the heart of the Santa Clara Valley's vineyard land lies the well known San Martin Vineyards Company. This family enterprise was owned for many years by the closely knit Filice family which originally came from the Province of Cosenza in Calabria, Italy and members of which are spread all over Central and Southern Europe. The Filice antecedents in the wine business are said to date back to around the year 1700.

A branch of the Filice family settled in California in the Santa Clara Valley in the early eighteen eighties and planted considerable land there in the early part of the century. In 1932 Bruno Filice, who also had wine interests in Italy, acquired the old San Martin Winery and Vineyards which had been founded forty years before. Since then a great many changes and improvements have been made in modernizing the winery and installing new equipment.

In 1972 the Filice family formed a new corporation with a New Orleans-based land development company, which planted 1,650 acres in nearby Monterey County, bringing the winery's total vineyard acreage to about 2,200. The winery was expanded dramatically in 1973, the same year San Martin began to release aged, vintage-dated varietals. The winery's large tasting room has become something of a landmark on U.S. Highway 101.

The corporation is headed by Calvin O. Waters, with Bruno Filice, John M. Filice Jr. and Michael J. Filice Jr. as vice presidents. The winemaker is Ed Friedrich.

A full line of table wines, sparkling wines, aperitif and dessert wines including vermouths and fruit wines are available, *San Martin* being the featured brand.

The *San Martin* bottle fermented sparkling wines include: *Brut* (very dry), *Extra Dry* (medium) and *Demi Sec* (fairly sweet) Champagne as well as Pink Champagne and Sparkling Burgundy. A specialty is the Spumante Moscato, a sparkling Muscat made by the traditional Italian method.

San Martin is the featured brand for the specially aged aperitif and dessert wines and for the Berry Wines made from fresh berries from the Santa Clara Valley: Strawberry Fraisette, Blackberry (Boysenberry Variety) and Loganberry.

Bertero Winery, Gilroy (Hecker Pass)

A winery in the western foothills of the Santa Clara Valley in the Hecker Pass area.

Alfonso Bertero, the founder, was born in the neighborhood of Turin in Italy and came to this country in 1911. He first worked for the Standard Oil Company and in 1919 went into the wine business, selling grapes to home wine makers and to other wineries for the production of sacramental wines. He moved to his present location in 1924, where he built the winery and his home. The property is part of the old Los Alamos grant and some of the original Spanish wooden stakes survive.

Bertero, who has since passed away, turned the family enterprise over before he died to his son Angelo, who in turn is aided by his sons, Angelo Jr. and Carl.

In 1973 the Berteros built a "pavilion" tasting room, with facilities for winery tours, picnics and private tastings for groups up to 100.

Table wines only are produced, all from local grapes. Burgundy is available as well as Sauterne (from the French Colombard grape). Varietals include Pinot Noir, Cabernet Sauvignon, Barbera, Zinfandel, Grignolino, Chardonnay and Semillon. Outstanding is the winery's Grenache Rosé, made exclusively from that grape. *Bertero* is the winery's main brand.

Bonesio Winery, Gilroy (Uvas district)

A winery well known in the surrounding counties, producing sound "country" Santa Clara table wines. It is located in the hilly Uvas district west of Gilroy near the Hecker Pass, *uvas* being Spanish for grapes and the region so named because the Spaniards, presumably, already raised or found grapes there. The property forms part of the former Solis Rancho, and the Bonesio residence, over a hundred years old, was once the headquarters of the large Solis Rancho grant.

Pietro (Peter) Bonesio, the founder of the winery, came from an Italian wine making family and was born in Cardona near Asti in Piedmont, Italy. He came to the United States in 1903 and worked in subway construction in New York City. He later farmed in Louisiana and then moved to Oakland, California, where he was engaged in the concrete business. In 1915 he reverted to the traditional family occupation, first starting a winery in the Rucker district, north of Gilroy. In 1921 Peter Bonesio bought the 600-acre Solis Rancho which has been the family home since.

Peter Bonesio lived until 1966, but turned the business over to his sons, Louis and Victor, in 1932. In the early 1970s the winery was acquired by Varietal Vintners Inc., headed by Daniel Hazelton, and storage capacity reached 175,000 gallons. The winemaker is John Gordon.

The Bonesio specialties include Grenache Rosé, Emerald Riesling, White Malvasia, Grignolino, Cabernet Sauvignon and Zinfandel.

The winery bottles under various labels, but the *Uvas* brand label is used for their finer wines.

Rapazzini's Los Altos Winery, Gilroy

Founded in 1963 by Angelo Rapazzini and his two sons, Jon and Victor, this company at first restricted its retail sales to the winery just south of Gilroy. During the next decade the family earned a reputation for well-made, fully-aged table wines, and following the death of their father, Jon and Victor made the decision to go into national distribution.

Angelo and Vita Rapazzini, from the time they came to the Santa Clara Valley from their native Italy, had dreamed of owning a winery. It was not until their two sons were grown, however, that the family was able to acquire an inactive, 42-year-old winery on the outskirts of town. Depending on word-of-mouth rather than advertising, the Rapazzinis built a large clientele, reportedly serving more than a million tastings at the winery in 10 years.

There are 10 *Rapazzini* varietals offered, including limited production Pinot Noir and Cabernet Sauvignon. The others are French Colombard, Green Hungarian, Emerald Gold (from the Emerald Riesling grape), Chenin Blanc, Barbera, Zinfandel, Carignane and Grenache Rosé. The reds are aged in redwood and then white oak. The Barbera released in 1973 was a non-vintage blend averaging seven years in age.

SANTA CRUZ COUNTY

Bargetto's Santa Cruz Winery, Soquel

Founders of this family firm were the brothers Philip and John Bargetto, sons of Giuseppe Bargetto, wine grower and winemaker from the neighborhood of Asti in Piedmont, Italy. Giuseppe came to this country but then returned to his native land. His sons, however, both came over to stay. Philip came in 1887 and worked for some twelve years in the old Delmas Winery near San Jose. John immigrated in 1909 and first engaged in the produce and grape shipping business. In 1933 Philip and John founded the Bargetto Winery in Soquel which was owned by John Bargetto until his death in 1964. It is now owned by his son Lawrence, the winemaker, chemist and general manager. Two daughters of Philip complete the family membership of the enterprise.

The Bargetto wines are produced from grapes purchased from vineyards scattered over Santa Cruz and Santa Clara counties. Table wines are the specialty while aperitif and dessert wines round out the line.

In addition to the usual generic types, the following *Bargetto* varietals are available: Pinot Chardonnay, Pinot Blanc, Sauvignon Blanc, Chenin Blanc (sweet), Flora, Zinfandel Rosé, Zinfandel, Barbera, Ruby Cabernet and Pinot Noir. The winery also produces an interesting dry Muscat and a Moscato Amabile, and Johannisberg Riesling and Sylvaner were added to the list in the spring of 1975.

In the early 1970s the Bargetto Winery sold its *Winemaster* label for generic wines and began bottling a line of less expensive table wines under the *Santa Cruz Cellars* brand. These were extremely well received, especially the Chablis and Zinfandel, and can be found in many better wine and gourmet shops.

Nicasio Vineyards, Soquel

This winery owned and run by Dan Wheeler is located some six miles north of Soquel near Santa Cruz. After three years of home wine making Wheeler bonded Nicasio Vineyards in 1955.

Dan started wine making in the belief that fine wines should be 100% varietal, free of sulphur dioxide and stored at an even temperature the year around. To provide a perfect nest for his wines he started, back in 1952, to dig a cave into a sandstone hill down the road a little from his home. It is gradually being enlarged and is composed of two rooms devoted to storage and tasting purposes with an average temperature of 58 degrees F., varying but little throughout the year.

The winery may be small but the devotion inspiring it is as great as its wines are fine.

A nearby vineyard is planted to Johannisberg (White) Riesling, Chardonnay, Zinfandel and Pinot Noir. The Wheeler wines are made from these grapes and from Pinot noir obtained from hillside vineyards near Soquel. They also produce a Rosé made from Zinfandel and bottle fermented Champagne, with no dosage added at all, of the French *Nature* type, very dry but without harshness, made from the White Riesling, Chardonnay and Pinot Noir grapes, and produce and market a Chardonnay table wine.

For Dan, a senior engineer of an electronic manufacturing company, the winery is also a retirement plan but far more than just a hobby.

The packaging of the Wheeler wines is elegant, in keeping with the contents. Besides the Champagne *Nature*, the following vintage table wines are available in small quantities from the winery and by mail order:

WHITE: Johannisberg Riesling, Chardonnay, Sylvaner;
RED: Cabernet Sauvignon, Zinfandel;
ROSÉ: Zinfandel Rosé.

The Nicasio Vineyards wine labels are distinctive and individually signed. The brand reads: *Wine by Wheeler.*

Roudon-Smith Vineyards, Santa Cruz

The first wine of Roudon-Smith Vineyards, a 1972 Sauvignon Blanc from grapes grown near Hollister, was released as winemaker Bob Roudon was making four new 1973 wines. The Hollister Sauvignon Blanc was aged in two batches, one in French oak and the other in Canadian oak. The two were bottled separately to give consumers a chance to detect the subtle differences in the wood.

The winery was founded in 1972 by Roudon and his partner, James Smith. They planted a 12-acre vineyard in the Santa Cruz Mountains. Eventually they planned to release Pinot Noir, Cabernet Sauvignon, Barbera and Chenin Blanc, in addition to later vintages of Sauvignon Blanc from Hollister and another from Sonoma County vineyards.

The production remains small, and Roudon makes his wines with as little cellar treatment as possible, including filtration or fining. Thus all of them, including the whites, will normally throw some sediment. This could present a problem for the unwary, used to crystal-clear California white wines, who fail to pour them properly.

E. *MONTEREY, SAN LUIS OBISPO AND SANTA BARBARA COUNTIES*

Monterey County

As mentioned toward the beginning of this book, the vineyard acreage of Monterey County has skyrocketed to the point where the region has become one of the state's most important viticultural areas. An example is the founding in 1972 of International Vineyards, which now has 1,380 acres planted at Chular and Greenfield.

The company is owned by Gold Seal Vineyards Inc.—one of the largest wine producers in New York's Finger Lakes District.

Chalone Vineyard, Soledad

This small winery, owned by a corporation founded in 1965 and reorganized in 1970, began making wines in 1966. They are of very high quality.

The property is the former F.W. Silvear Vineyard, the owner of which died in 1957. It passed through different hands until the first 160 acres was purchased by the company now known as Gavilan Vineyards Inc., headed by Dick Graff as president and winemaker and Phil Woodward as vice president. New acreage was added, and the land now totals 480 acres of which 125 are planted to vines, mostly Chardonnay and Pinot Noir. In 1974 a new winery was built, including an underground barrel storage area.

The *Chalone Vineyard* wines, all aged in small Limousin oak barrels in the manner of the classic French Burgundies, are Chardonnay, Pinot Blanc, Chenin Blanc and Pinot Noir.

Visitors are welcome, but the owners ask that advance appointments be made by writing to the winery in Soledad or by telephoning the company's business office in San Francisco.

The Monterey Vineyard (Monterey Bay Co.), Gonzales

Founded in 1971, the Monterey Vineyard rapidly became the county's largest grower, with over 9,600 acres planted by associated vineyards on both the lower slopes of the Gavilan Heights and the Santa Lucia Mountains.

Each site was selected to take advantage of climate and soil, and only fine varietals were planted, including Pinot Noir, Gamay Beaujolais, Petite Sirah, Chardonnay, Johannisberg Riesling and Sauvignon Blanc. The Paloma Ranch is believed to be the largest single planting of Cabernet Sauvignon in the world.

A large new winery began operations at Gonzales with the 1974 crush, but the first *Monterey Vineyard* wines had already been introduced in New York and other major American markets. The wines, made by Dr. Richard Peterson of the Monterey Vineyard, are sold by the associated Monterey Bay Co., headed by Gerald Asher, a former British wine merchant and an internationally known authority on the wines of the world.

SAN LUIS OBISPO COUNTY

As the growers of grapes and the makers of wine have retreated before the march of civilization and overpopulation, the central coast of California has started to come back as a major winegrowing area. The dramatic growth of vineyard acreage in Monterey County already has been discussed, and San Luis Obispo County to the south, important for its fine wines in the nineteenth century, is experiencing a similar renaissance, from 379 acres in 1964 to 3,250 a decade later. Agricultural experts say there are at least 30,000 acres of potential vineyard land in the county, ranging in climate from very cool, as in parts of Sonoma and Mendocino Counties, to very warm, similar to the Central Valley and Southern California.

In spite of the "newness" of many of the vineyards here, winemaking goes back to the mission days. One very active family operation, the Rotta Winery at Templeton, was founded in 1856 when a Frenchman named Siot planted the first vines there. It is now run by Mervin Rotta, whose family has owned it since 1907.

Hoffman Mountain Ranch Vineyards (Hoffman's Mountain Winery), Paso Robles

For 23 years Dr. Stanley Hoffman was a successful internist and heart specialist in Los Angeles, on the staff of many hospitals and on the clinical staff at the UCLA medical school. In 1960 he bought a 1,200-acre ranch at an altitude of nearly 2,000 feet in the mountains west of Paso Robles, about 15 miles from the ocean. At first he planted nut orchards, but as his interest in fine wines grew, he decided to grow wine grapes. As of 1975 Hoffman Mountain Ranch had about 100 acres in Cabernet Sauvignon, Pinot Noir, Gamay, Chardonnay and Sylvaner, with planned expansion already under--way. The vines are tended and the wine is made with the advice of the peripatetic Andre Tchelistcheff, consultant to so many of the state's premium wineries.

In January of 1974, after a stint as a teaching cardiologist at the Hammersmith Hospital in London, Dr. Hoffman moved with his family from Beverly Hills to the ranch at Paso Robles and turned his career around—from practicing physician and part-time wine-grower to full-time vintner and part-time doctor (although being the only cardiologist in an area of 20,000 people bodes badly for the term "part-time"). Most of the grapes from the early harvests were sold to Mirassou, but in 1972 the first *Hoffman Mountain* wine, a Pinot Noir made by Dr. Hoffman's son, David, was made. It was followed in later years by Chardonnay, Cabernet Sauvignon and Pinot Noir.

The wines are made in the classic French tradition, and some of the first released were well-received not only in California but England as well.

Pesenti Winery, Templeton

A small, family operation founded in 1934 by Frank Pesenti, this winery nonetheless has won many awards at the Los Angeles County and California State Fairs for the quality of its products.

Frank Pesenti, now in partnership with his son, Victor, and son-in-law, Aldo Nerelli, still is active. *Pesenti* wines include the normal generics, as well as Cabernet, Zinfandel and Zinfandel Rosé. Notable among the whites is Chateau D'Oro, a light, sweet table wine, and Chateau Blanc, medium sweet. The wines of this company are sold only in the local area, where they have earned a just reputation, and from the winery tasting room off U. S. Highway 101.

York Mountain Winery, Templeton

Representative of good wine making in San Luis Obispo County is the York Winery, owned and operated by Max Goldman and located just below the peak of York Mountain on the eastern slopes of the Santa Lucia Mountains overlooking Templeton and the valley below.

The ranch property was acquired in 1882 by Andrew York. Born in Indiana Andrew came out West from Missouri in the eighteen fifties and settled in San Luis Obispo County after first having spent some time in the Napa Valley. A proud family possession is the original deed to the land, dated 1875, made out to Jacob B. Grandstaff from whom Andrew bought it, and signed by U. S. Grant, President of the United States.

Andrew York found that the grape vines he had planted to supplement his apple orchard yielded more grapes than he could market and so, with the help of his sons, Walter, Thomas and Silas, built a small winery to take care of the surplus. Shortly after the turn of the century additional land was purchased and a large vineyard planted of Zinfandels, selected because they mature early and thereby usually miss the early winter frosts. About that time too the winery was enlarged with the use of bricks molded and burned on the place in the ancient tradition of the Babylonians.

The York place is a historic one, as times goes, and many tales are told of how the lumber to build the original houses and winery was carted over the rough and steep mountain roads all the way from Cayucos on Estero Bay which at that time was a small flourishing harbor before the railroad came to Templeton. Indians used trails running through the property and camped overnight on the mountain on their way to the hot sulphur and mud baths in what is now Paso Robles, twelve miles distant. Nearby also is the San Ygnacio Ranch, established by Ignace Jan Paderewski, the great Polish patriot and world famous pianist, who raised wine grapes and had them crushed at the York Winery.

After the death of Andrew in 1913 his sons Walter and Silas took over the family enterprise which became the York Brothers Winery. Upon their retirement in 1944 the third generation wine makers, Wilfrid and Howard, continued the operation until 1954 from which time Wilfrid ran it in sole proprietorship until 1970.

The new owner, Max Goldman, bought the winery after 39 years as a winemaker, chemist and executive in California and New York. He will continue to produce the award-winning *York Mountain* Zinfandel, and will add a Champagne to be produced from new plantings of Chardonnay and Pinot Noir. He has also planted Cabernet Sauvignon, and has refurbished the building, adding a tasting room.

Goldman planted a total of 95 acres to varietals, leaving, as he said, "the balance of the 207-acre parcel for the deer and the wild turkey."

SANTA BARBARA COUNTY

Santa Barbara Winery, Santa Barbara

Established in 1962 by architect and enophile Pierre Lafond, Santa Barbara Winery planted its first vineyards, 40 acres in the Santa Ynez Valley, in 1971. Prior to that Lafond, who is his own winemaker, made table and fruit wines from grapes and berries purchased from other growers in Monterey and San Luis Obispo Counties.

The first wines from the winery's own vineyards were scheduled for release in 1976. Previously only two Sherries and a 1968 Zinfandel had been offered under the *Santa Barbara Winery* label, with an additional Sherry, a Tawny Port and a Cabernet Sauvignon also to be released in 1976. Since 1965 Lafond has made sound generics and some varietals under the *Mission* label, and they have been extremely popular in hotels and restaurants. Sparkling wines are offered under the *Gold Rush* label, and *Solvang*, named for the small Danish community northwest of Santa Barbara, is the brand for fruit wines and mead.

XII

THE GREAT INLAND VALLEY REGION

*T*HIS VAST VALLEY region sweeps down in a fairly narrow band parallel to the coast line, from which it is separated by the mountains of the Coast Range. Some three hundred miles long, it stretches from north of the city of Sacramento down south beyond Bakersfield in Kern County. Its climate, moderately warm in the northern areas, becomes progressively hotter the farther south one comes.

The region takes in the territory of both the Sacramento and the San Joaquin river valleys. It is the home of the great California aperitif and dessert wine production, for which the climate and soil are especially well suited. Most of the vines are cultivated by irrigation.

From north to south we have the *Lodi-Sacramento,* the *Escalon-Modesto,* and the *Fresno-San Joaquin Valley* districts.

There are many winery names in this huge region, some famous because of their size, some because of the unusual quality of the wines they produce in the warm climate. Some sturdy table wines have only local reputations while others, mass produced, are for sale in every state in the union.

A number of the active wineries in the valley are old ones, such as the Golden State Winery at Fresno, founded in 1908 and a specialist in sparkling wines, and the Cadlolo Winery at Escalon, in business since 1913.

Many were founded after Repeal, such as Alex's Winery and Coloma Wine Cellars, started in Lodi in 1935 by a Greek named Christ Alexander; Delicato Vineyards of Manteca, established in 1935 and now producing nine million gallons a year; Pirrone Wine Cellars, founded at Manteca in 1936 by Frank Pirrone and now operated by his son, Alfred, a graduate in food technology from the University of California; the A. Nonini Winery founded in 1935 at Fresno, and Nicholas G. Verry Inc., founded in 1933, located at Parlier since 1942 and producer of Greek-type wines such as Retsina and Philery.

There also are many wineries of more recent origin. The Lockford Vintner Corp. at Lodi dates back to 1946. The Cribari Vineyard at Fresno bears the name of one of California's oldest vineyard families but was established in 1966. Also recent is the Landis Vineyard of Fresno, which specializes in Sherries. In 1972 the old Cherokee Winery at Acampo was purchased from the California Wine Association by a Southern California company and renamed Montcalm Vintners, but by 1974 it was being reorganized by members of the Filice family from Santa Clara County.

A. *LODI—SACRAMENTO DISTRICT*

This district takes in the wine producing areas of Sacramento County and of the northern part of San Joaquin County.

In Sacramento County there is a wine growing area which stretches east of the city of Sacramento down southward, where both table and dessert wines are produced. Elk Grove is a center famous for its production of berry and fruit wines.

Northern San Joaquin County contains the famed wine growing district of Lodi, which spreads out to a surrounding region some ten miles deep. Lodi is on the Mokelumne River, which flows into the

San Joaquin and is sometimes referred to as lying in the upper reaches of the San Joaquin Valley. It can also be said to be situated at the juncture of the Sacramento and San Joaquin valleys and in what is known as the Central Valley.

Lodi, recognized as a separate viticultural district, is especially noted for its aperitif and dessert wines. It is the center of a vast Flame Tokay vineyard district, spectacular in the fall due to the brilliant coloring of the grapes. The Flame Tokays are mainly used as table grapes, but are also employed in many of the dessert wines produced by the Lodi wineries including the wine called tokay.

To the north of Sacramento, in Butte and Tehama Counties, there has been a resurgence of wine growing in a warm region that was an important vineyard area in the last century, and which continued to produce wine until Prohibition. This was the area called Vina, where Leland Stanford planted vineyards that ultimately covered 3,500 acres along the Sacramento River, and where the first wine grapes were planted before the Civil War by Peter Lassen. Although technically it is not part of the Lodi-Sacramento District, we have tampered with geography a little to include it here for convenience.

BUTTE COUNTY DISTRICT

Butte Creek Vineyards, Chico

This is one of the growing number of California wineries with women winemakers, in this case Dr. Marian Baldy, one of the six people who founded the business in 1972. So far only three wines have been released, all 100% varietals: French Colombard, an unusually dry and very pleasant Gamay Rosé and a Ruby Cabernet aged in French oak cooperage. By the time the winery reaches its maximum size in 1980, it is anticipated another red and white will have been added to the list.

The winery was established in an old dairy by Frank Pangburn, its president, his wife, Barbara, Dick and Marian Baldy and Bill and Virginia Linder. Marian Baldy, who has a doctorate in genetics, teaches at Chico State University along with her husband and Linder.

The wines, which are made from purchased grapes in small lots with great care and technical skill, already have reached some distant markets.

SACRAMENTO—ELK GROVE DISTRICT

Gibson Wine Company, Elk Grove

Robert H. Gibson, founder of the company, turned to the production of wines after first having been a successful stockbroker both in his home town of Cincinnati, Ohio, and in New York City.

He felt that many people would enjoy wines made from other fruit than grapes and experimented for some years in the production of berry and fruit wines. His faith was fully justified and he succeeded in developing a large market for his products. Berry and fruit wines have come into their own (see Chapter IX) and the Gibson Wine Company has become one of the largest producers in this field.

Robert Gibson, Bob as he was known to his friends, spent much of his time in Roseville, California, where he had a large cattle ranch and raised rare pheasants as a hobby. It is not surprising therefore that the trademark of the corporation is the *Golden Pheasant* which appears on many of its labels and is blown into most of its bottles. Bob Gibson died in 1960.

The Elk Grove Gibson Winery, where all of the company's berry and fruit wines, as well as the table and aperitif and dessert wines are produced, was originally a gas engine works. In 1934 it was converted into a winery, Robert Gibson acquiring the property in 1943. From a small plant it grew into a modern and up to date winery, producing some of the best known berry and fruit wines in California.

The Gibson Wine Company is now owned by a cooperative, formerly the Sanger Winery Association of Sanger. Jake Rheingans is the president, Bud Jones the vice president and Alex Farafontoff is winemaker.

The *Gibson's Old Fashioned* brand is used for the berry and fruit wines.

Gibson's Premium Select is the featured brand for the usual table and aperitif and dessert wines. *Vinesse* is used for the Champagne and Cold Duck.

LODI DISTRICT
(Northern San Joaquin County)

Barengo Vineyards, Acampo

This winery has had a checkered ownership since it was founded in 1935 as the Acampo Winery. In 1973 Dino Barengo, who had owned it for nearly 30 years, sold it for $2,000,000 to Winkler-Scheid Corp. (now called Winkler-Scheid Vineyards, Inc.), a diversified investment firm that had been involved in vineyard management, plastics, small appliances and color graphics. Barengo remained as a consultant.

In addition to expanding Barengo Vineyards and increasing its output, the corporation owns or manages over 3,100 acres of vineyard through its Monterey Farming Corp. in the Greenfield-King City area of Monterey County, a region pioneered by Mirassou Vineyards and which has seen new plantings by wineries such as Almadén, Paul Masson and Wente Bros.

Barengo has been associated with the Acampo Winery since the early forties, when it was a stock corporation of which Cesare Mondavi, who later took over the Charles Krug Winery, was president. In 1943 the Acampo Winery was acquired by the Gibson Wine Company, now of Elk Grove, and Dino Barengo managed it for that concern. Barengo then leased the winery and finally purchased it in 1946, when he became the sole proprietor.

Both table and aperitif or dessert wines of sound standard quality are produced, with *Barengo, Barengo Reserve* and *Barengo Cellars* the featured brands.

East-Side Winery, Lodi

This well known winery, one of the largest in the district, is a farmers' co-operative, founded in 1934. Its name was adopted because the area East of Lodi where the winery is located is known for its particularly rich soil yielding high quality grapes.

The co-operative is formed by 130 growing farmer-stockholders to whom all returns are made after costs and taxes have been paid. Ole R. Mettler is president of the co-op, Leon Kirschenmann vice president and Ernest C. Haas general manager.

The regular types of generic table and of aperitif and dessert wines are produced with *Royal Host* the featured brand. Brandy, under the same label, is an important specialty.

In 1962, after a great deal of study, East-Side entered the premium wine field, with well-aged aperitif wines and several varietals, including Chenin Blanc, Grey Riesling, Semillon, Emerald Riesling, Gold and Ruby Cabernet, the latter three made from new California grapes developed by the University of California at Davis.

Guild Wineries and Distilleries, Lodi

Formerly known as the Wine Growers Guild and later the Guild Wine Company, the official name of this enterprise is now Guild Wineries and Distilleries. It is a cooperative of wineries owned by about 1,000 individual growers, and is the third-largest wine producer in the United States, with an aggregate storage capacity at all its facilities of over 50,000,000 gallons.

Most of the wines are finished and bottled at Lodi, but are made at seven producing wineries from Lodi in the north to Delano in the south. On March 1, 1971, Guild acquired the California wine brands and inventories of Schenley, including Roma at Fresno and the historic Cresta Blanca brand originally from Livermore, as well as the Schenley wineries at Fresno and Delano.

Cresta Blanca was moved to Ukiah, where it is operated as a subsidiary, specializing in wines made from grapes grown in Mendocino County.

Although the Guild cooperative was not formed until World War II, it is or has been successor to some of the oldest and best-known names in the American wine industry: Alta Winery, Cameo Vineyards, A. Mattei and B. Cribari and Sons, the Italian Vineyard Co. founded in 1883 by Secundo Guasti, and Garrett & Co., the huge firm headed by Captain Paul Garrett that once had wineries and thousands of acres of vines in California, New York and North Carolina.

Today, in addition to the central blending and bottling cellars at Lodi, Guild has the Bear Creek Winery at Lodi, the Del Rio Winery at Woodbridge nearby, the Fresno, McCall and Roma Wineries at Fresno and the L.K. Marshall Winery at Delano.

L. K. Marshall, one of the great men in the history of California wine, was president of Guild from its inception in 1943 until his retirement in 1957. He died soon after. Hubert Mettler is now chairman of the board. Guild's president is Robert M. Ivie, a Stanford graduate active in all phases of the wine industry who, as a hobby, experiments growing varietals at his home in Atherton. The vice president in charge of production is W. E. Kite.

The regular types of table wines and of aperitif and dessert wines including vermouth are marketed under the *Winemasters Guild* brand, the table wine for which the company is best known being the familiar "Vino da Tavola," a sweet red table wine of the Vino Rosso order, launched by the company as a new type of wine back in 1950.

The most celebrated products under the *Ceremony* label are undoubtedly the company's straight dry Brandies, 5 and 8 years old, the latter being considered by many an expert to be one of the finest and smoothest brandies produced in California. The *Guild* "Blue Ribbon" Brandy is a blended and sweetened product similar in character to the majority of California brandies marketed. It should be noted that all the Guild Wine Company's brandies are produced from the Tokay grape for which the Lodi district is famous and which lends itself well for brandy distillation.

Other Guild Wine Co. brands used in various parts of the United States include:

Table and dessert wines: *Roma, Cresta Blanca, Garrett, Famiglia Cribari, Mendocino, J. Pierrot* and *La Boheme;*

Sparkling wines: *Winemaster's Guild, Tres Grand, Cook's, Cribari, Jeanne D'Arc, Versailles, La Boheme, Roma* and *J. Pierrot;*

Brandy: *Roma, St. Mark* and *Citation.*

B. *ESCALON—MODESTO DISTRICT*

This district covers the wine growing areas and wineries of the southern part of San Joaquin County, from Stockton south and southeast to Manteca and Escalon; it takes in Stanislaus County from Salida on down to Modesto and also includes the Livingston area in northern Merced County.

The Escalon-Modesto district, located in the northern San Joaquin Valley, is best known for its dessert wines, but table and sparkling wines are also produced. Some of the California wineries with the largest distribution are located in this district.

Franzia Brothers Winery, Ripon

This corporation, located about halfway between the towns of
Manteca and Escalon in the southernmost part of San Joaquin
County, was purchased in 1973 by the Coca-Cola Bottling Co. of
New York. It was sold by the sons of the late Giuseppe Franzia
(Joe Sr.), a native of Genoa, Italy, who first settled in San Francisco
and then moved to Stockton. He bought the Franzia ranch in Ripon
in 1906, and was prominent in the wine business from 1933 until his
death in 1952.

Giuseppe Franzia's sons carried on the family business for many
years and one of them, Joseph Jr., is president of the new company.
Winemaking at Franzia continues to be a family affair, with Louis
Quaccia succeeding his father, Fernando, as winemaker and chemist.

Franzia produces and markets sound, standard-quality wines at
popular prices, virtually all of it from grapes grown in the San
Joaquin Valley. Today it is the fifth-largest winery in California,
with 4,000 acres of vineyard under its control and a storage capacity
of 20,000,000 gallons.

MODESTO DISTRICT
(Stanislaus County)

E. & J. Gallo Winery, Modesto

One of the biggest marketing stories in the wine industry in
1974 was the news that Ernest and Julio Gallo, who already sold
about 40% of the wine drunk in the United States, were introducing
a new line of varietal wines in cork-finished, lead foil-capsuled

bottles. That they were serious about these new wines—French Colombard, Sauvignon Blanc, Chenin Blanc, Barbera, Ruby Cabernet and Zinfandel, as well as a California Riesling and a Rosé—can be gauged by the fact their first order for corks reportedly was for 50,000,000.

As with everything else they do, their decision to enter the so-called "premium" field was not a hasty one. It resulted from 10 years of vineyard research, market studies and experimental wine-making.

In 40 years the Gallo brothers' winery grew from a tiny operation at Modesto to the world's largest winery. That in itself is worth some consideration here. But also they are responsible, as much as anyone, for the doubling of wine consumption in this country in the past decade, to over 2.6 gallons per year per adult, still pitifully small compared with nations such as France, Italy and Spain.

Along with many others the Gallos studied this matter for years, trying to learn why Americans drink so little wine in comparison with some of those other countries, all the more surprising as the United States ranks among the larger wine growing countries of the world.

Ernest Gallo came to the conclusion that there are at least three reasons why consumption is so much greater in the foreign countries mentioned:

1. The wines of those countries are made more to the liking of their peoples than are American wines made to the American taste;

2. Wines in foreign countries are priced to encourage their widespread use in volume;

3. Wine is displayed to suggest frequent use in volume.

Guided by these basic reasons the full resources of the Gallo research organization at the winery were—and are—devoted to the development of wines that will mean to Americans what Spanish wine means to the Spaniards, Italian wine means to the Italians and French wine means to the French.

It is certain that the Gallo brothers remain dedicated to their objective, undertaken when they founded their winery in 1933, to provide American homes with good, sound wines at popular prices. They attribute their progress towards that goal to the company's continuous scientific research for new, modern ways to improve the efficiency of grape growing and of wine making and to enhance the taste appeal of wines for American consumers.

One of the keys to Gallo's growth is the company's view that because wines are perishable, the only way to establish wine as a staple beverage in the American diet is to make certain (or as certain as humanly possible) that the consumer will be fully satisfied with every bottle purchased. This is why Gallo wines are bottled only at the winery where they are made and sealed under supervision of the company's own expert enologists in Gallo's exclusive "Flavor-Guard" bottles.

This bottle is the reason why the Gallo family in 1958, at a cost of more than six million dollars, built their own glass factory adjoining the Gallo Winery at Modesto. The glass, it is stated, protects the wine from the effects of ultra violet light rays. Gallo, it is believed, is the only winery in the world to manufacture its own bottles.

Gallo's research begins with the grapes. In the Gallo vineyards in Stanislaus and Merced Counties a large number of grape varieties are grown which the company constantly tests for its blends of wine while Gallo's viticulturists also guide other growers in producing grapes for the company.

Gallo's wines are made from grapes grown in the viticultural districts where they thrive best. In addition to the original Gallo winery at Modesto there are Gallo Cellars at Fresno and Livingston and several grower-owned wineries in Napa and Sonoma Counties producing wine for the company under the latter's supervision.

Convinced by many years of research that glass-lined steel tanks are preferable, Gallo has adopted that method of cooperage, using what are virtually giant bottles.

Modesto, the home of Gallo wines, is in the heart of the historic County of Stanislaus with its wine growing tradition dating back to about 1854 when George H. Krause, a native of Germany, laid out what was to become his famed Red Mountain Vineyard on part of the old Mexican grant El Rancheria del Rio Stanislaus.

It was in Modesto in 1933, the last year of Prohibition, that the Gallo brothers visualized the coming rebirth of the California wine industry, dormant during the dry years. They thought of creating a modern winery and planned that some day homes throughout the nation would proudly serve wines from shiny bottles bearing their name.

It was an ambitious plan for the brothers. Ernest was twenty-four and Julio a year younger. They had been brought up in the tradition of good wine, born as they were in the third generation of a wine growing family whose forebears had cultivated vineyards and made wine in Italy's famed Province of Piedmont. The Gallo brothers had been educated in the public schools of Modesto and knew about viti-culture firsthand, having worked in the family's vineyards. They borrowed and scraped together enough dollars to rent a warehouse in Modesto to house a few casks and a grape crusher to serve as a winery until they could build one of their own. In that old ware-house the first Gallo vintage was crushed and fermented that same year, 1933, a historic one in the Gallo story.

A few months later they built a small wine cellar on the outskirts of Modesto. This first concrete structure on the banks of Dry Creek was carefully planned as the first unit of the winery the Gallo broth-ers envisioned. It was built and ready for use in 1935.

At first the Gallos made only red table wines, selling them in bulk to wholesale bottlers. In 1937 they were able to build an extension to their cellar and to install further equipment. They began to produce port, sherry and muscatel in addition to their table wines. They studied modern developments in viticulture and wine making and searched for the best types of cooperage and other winery equipment. Julio Gallo devoted himself increasingly to the development of the most suitable grape varieties in the family's vineyards and to the production of wines while Ernest Gallo studied consumer and trade problems and marketing.

In the Gallo vineyards at Modesto, which the family had owned since 1925, new varieties were grafted onto old rootstocks. Additional vines were planted to grow the choicer varieties suited to local and climatic conditions. Gradually the Gallos increased their vineyard acreage, planting vines in the Keyes district of Stanislaus County and acquiring a vineyard near Livingston in Merced County.

The Gallo brothers realized that Fresno and the Southern San Joaquin Valley region yielded grape varieties most desirable for the sweeter dessert wines while Napa and Sonoma in the Northern Coastal Counties provided the best grapes for dry table wines. Accordingly they selected grapes from these districts to complete their assortment of wines.

It was not until 1940 that the Gallos felt they were producing wines of the quality they wanted to market in bottles bearing the family label. It was in that year, another milestone in the Gallo saga, when their wines first appeared on the market. A following of consumers soon developed and Gallo advertising began.

From a small beginning in California and Louisiana the *Gallo* wines gained a steady and increasing acceptance. The company concentrated on trying to please the consumer. The Gallo brothers and their staff interviewed buyers of their wines to learn the exact characteristics of wine flavor, of dryness or sweetness and of color that would please householders. They talked to retailers and salesmen to learn what their customers wanted and they strove to get their wines efficiently displayed and stocked. Year after year they were introduced in additional markets from coast to coast and their sales continued to grow.

There is no doubt that the Gallos have contributed and are contributing much to making wine ever more popular as a national beverage in the United States.

By the mid-70s Gallo was marketing more than 50 types of wine, all bottled at their Modesto winery. Over 30 were of the traditional types, led by the most popular generic table wines, the usual types of aperitif and dessert wine including vermouths and berry wines, Boone's Farm Apple Wine and Concord Grape. In addition there are Vin Rosé, "Paisano" the popular wine of the Vino Rosso order, and "Pink Chablis," one of their most successful.

In 1968 *Old Decanter* brand Livingston Cream Sherry was added, named for the Livingston vineyard in Merced County. In 1969 they added *E. & J. Gallo* and *André* bulk fermented champagnes. Recently a new $1,500,000 headquarters building was erected at Modesto.

In 1957 Gallo launched its flavored aperitif wine "Thunderbird" which rapidly became very popular. In 1959 "Gypsy Rose," a pink aperitif, was introduced.

Here we see clearly the Gallo philosophy at work, that of introducing altogether new wines, specifically suited, it is hoped, to the American taste and thereby capturing a large market of their own. So far, they have been remarkably successful and there can be no doubt that the Gallos are smart merchandisers.

No doubt more new wines will be produced and launched by the energetic Gallos seeking to please the American palate. One great advantage of having successful proprietary names is to have consumers guided back to one's products, the aim being not only to produce new wines but also to create a captive market.

C. *THE MOTHER LODE*

The Mother Lode is the name traditionally applied to the historic Gold Rush country of the Sierra foothills, stretching 250 miles from Mariposa east of Merced, north to Downieville in Sierra County. It has never been regarded as one of California's classic wine-growing regions, but some wineries, such as the previously mentioned Coloma Wine Cellars, are well over a century old. These are a few representative samples.

TUOLUMNE COUNTY

Butler Winery, Sonora

Completed in 1970 after three years of construction, this winery was founded by J. L. Butler with his two sons, Roger and Marcus, as winemaker and sales manager respectively. Although it has a Sonora mailing address, the winery actually is located in the quiet forest behind Twain Harte, near Cedar Ridge. The younger Butlers purchased their father's interest and now operate as partners.

They make only red table wines, including two rosés, from grapes harvested in specially selected vineyards. Their best so far seems to be the Zinfandel which, like all Butler wines, is naturally clarified without filtration. The storage capacity is only 10,000 gallons, all in small oak casks.

Also produced is a unique fruit wine from the wild elderberries that grow in the foothills.

AMADOR COUNTY

D'Agostini Winery, Plymouth

Since 1911, the year the D'Agostinis took over the vineyards laid out by a Swiss immigrant named Adam Uhlinger in 1856, a cadre of loyal consumers has been trekking to the old stone winery northeast of Plymouth to buy hearty red wines.

In often harsh weather, the 125 acres of hillside vines surrounded by dense woods are tended by Armenio D'Agostini and his brothers, Tulio, Michele and Henry.

Several improvements and additions have been made since the time Uhlinger sold wine to the prospectors, and the winery is solidly prosperous. *D'Agostini* Burgundy and Zinfandel are the most popular.

Montevina, Plymouth

Located not far from the D'Agostini winery in the Shenandoah Valley, this winery was founded in 1973 by W. H. Field. The vineyards, some 80 years old, were acquired in 1970, and now Montevina farms includes 165 acres, about 35% of it in new vines. Nearly three-fourths of the grapes are Zinfandel, the balance being Cabernet Sauvignon, Barbera, Merlot, Sauvignon Blanc, Ruby Cabernet and Nebbiolo.

The first crush in 1973 yielded three Zinfandels, including a white and a *nouveau*, fermented by carbonic maceration and released right away. Production was doubled in 1974 after a new winery was built, and expansion continued in the second half of the decade. Nonetheless, Montevina continued to sell most of its grapes to other winemakers, reserving special lots for its own use. The winemaker is Gary Gott, and Dave Massoni is the vineyard manager.

EL DORADO COUNTY

Gold Hill Winery, Coloma

Another new winery, this one was founded by John and Beverly Hempt in 1969. Their seven-acre vineyard, a vestige of those days a century ago when the neighborhood boasted 3,700 acres of grape vines, is planted to Chenin blanc, Johannisberg Riesling and Cabernet Sauvignon. Aging wines are stored in small barrels of European and American oak.

A winemaker and vineyardist, Hempt was born in Europe and educated in Yugoslavia, Hungary, Germany and the United States. In addition to limited quantities of estate-bottled table wines (some of which won't be available for some time) the winery offers fruit and berry wines at its tasting room and gift shop in historic Coloma, the site of John Marshall's discovery of gold in 1848. Brands are *Gold Hill, Village Wines* and *Chateau René.*

D. *FRESNO—SAN JOAQUIN VALLEY DISTRICT*

This great district coincides with the lower San Joaquin Valley. It is famous especially for yielding wines of the sweeter dessert types, some of which have achieved great excellence. Table wines and bulk fermented sparkling wines are also produced.

The district takes in the following counties, from north to south: Madera, with the city of Madera the main sector;

Fresno, with its many famed wineries located in the city of Fresno and in the surrounding towns, with other famous wineries to be found in Sanger, Reedley, Parlier, Fowler, Selma and Kingsburg;

Kings, with its Hanford area;

Tulare, with the main winery centers in Dinuba, Cutler, Tulare, Lindsay, and on the Kern County line right across from Delano;

Kern, with Delano and the sector east of Bakersfield down to Arvin the wine production areas.

A number of well known wineries located in this district do not produce wines directly for the public under their own brands and are, for that reason only, not discussed in this *Guide*.

MADERA DISTRICT

Bisceglia Brothers Wine Co., Madera

This enterprise was founded in 1888 by four Bisceglia brothers, Joseph, Pasquale, Bruno and Alphonse, who came from a family of vineyardists and winemakers in Cosenza, Province of Calabria, Italy. They first settled in California in the Santa Clara Valley where they went into the wine business and also operated a large cannery. In 1939 the canning operation was discontinued and they directed their full attention to the wine business.

The large and modern winery was completed in 1947 and has a capacity of nearly eleven million gallons. Standard quality table, sparkling and aperitif and dessert wines are produced and distributed throughout the country.

The last of the original founders died in 1952, and the operation devolved to other members of the family. The winery is now a subsidiary of Canandaigua Wine Company of New York, although Bruno T. Bisceglia remains president.

Ficklin Vineyards, Madera

A small and unique operation, the only California winery specializing in port and the first winery in the United States that made port wines produced entirely from choice Portuguese grape varieties commercially available. The Ficklin Ports rate as the finest produced in California, being unsurpassed in quality and character with a full richness of flavor.

The Ficklin wine concern, founded in the middle of the nineteen forties, has made quite a name for itself and deservedly so. It is a family enterprise, the principal owners and operators being David (Dave) B. Ficklin, the winemaker and a well known wine judge, and his brother Walter C. Ficklin Jr., the vineyardist.

Their father, Walter C. Ficklin Sr., a charming gentleman familiar with all the better things of life, first came to California as a young man in 1911, making his home in Fresno County and planting his first vineyards and orchards in 1912. For many years he farmed grape and fruit ranches. In the early forties the family became interested in the idea of producing red dessert wines of top quality. They closely studied the Portuguese wine grape varieties which were being tested by the University of California under local growing conditions. The decision to establish a completely specialized vineyard complex and winery was the next step. Five of the finest Portuguese varieties were selected, Tinta Cão, Tinta Madeira, Alvarelhão, Souzao and Touriga, and the vineyards planted to them exclusively. A small but modern adobe winery was built by hand and 1948 saw the first vintage harvested.

Because the demand for these fine Ports has continually increased, the Ficklins increased their capacity in the mid-70s—but only slightly. Crushing facilities were modernized somewhat, but the winery remains much the same.

The greatest care is taken to produce the very best wines possible. The vineyards are meticulously tended to yield a limited crop of the choicest grapes. At harvest time the grape clusters are individually cut with small hand shears and all imperfect fruit is left on the vines.

They are first lightly crushed in stainless steel crushers, breaking the skins and separating them from the stems. The crushed grapes are transferred to small open vats where pure yeast culture is added. As soon as fermentation starts a wooden hand plunger is used to sub-merge and mix the skins with the juice, extracting thereby the full color and flavor of the grapes. The free-run juice is drawn off and the skins are given a further light pressing in a basket-type press, the resulting juice being added to the free-run for further flavor. At the proper stage of fermentation the juice is transformed into port wine by the addition of pure grape brandy. The wine is clarified naturally by gradual settling and racking in small oak puncheons or barrels. It is aged in oak for three years or longer and at least a further year in the bottle. Owing to this process, the Ficklin Ports, like those from Portugal, will throw a slight sediment, a sign of maturing and of age. The wines, therefore, should be poured carefully, so as not to disturb the deposit, or be decanted before serving. If disturbed, the bottle should be placed upright until the wine has had a chance to settle.

The main variety of Port available is the Tinta Port, a blend of the varieties grown. It is a full Ruby and is marketed under the *Ficklin Vineyards* brand.

A feature of the Ficklin operation is the use of a special pot still beverage brandy for the spirits addition. This gives the finished product considerable additional character, the wines possessing a harmonious bouquet and flavor when mature.

In addition there is a program of Special Bottlings of Vintage Ports, available only in small quantities direct from the winery.

The Ficklins have experimental plantings of Emerald Riesling and Ruby Cabernet, grape varieties developed by the University of California. Table wines have been produced on a pilot scale pro-gram, and only are available at the winery from time to time. The emphasis remains on producing what has been described by some experts as Ports among the finest in the world.

TULARE COUNTY

California Growers Winery Inc., Cutler

This co-operative winery was organized on April 20th 1936 and began operations at their present address on July first of the same year. It is owned and operated by growers who have been in the grape industry for many years.

From the beginning, the grower-members have required the personnel at the winery to produce quality wines and grape brandy. Part of the philosophy of California Growers Winery is that the farming interest of the growers, so important a part of the California and national agricultural picture, should be harmoniously balanced with those of the producer and the merchandiser of California wines.

The officers of California Growers are Robert Setrakian, president; Sam Balakian, vice president in charge of production, and Ramiro Jimenez, winemaker.

The company sells a full line of table, aperitif, dessert and sparkling wines as well as brandy under the following labels: *Growers, Maverick, Bounty, Tango, California Growers* and *Growers Frankenstein.*

KERN COUNTY

Although wine grapes date back to 1887, and the magnificent 10-foot-thick Emerson vine planted in 1892 still grows at an altitude of 4,000 feet in the Tehachapi Mountains, Kern County was known primarily for its oil wells until the agricultural explosion following the Korean War. In the 1960s growers, aided by the University of California, began to plant wine varieties such as Emerald Riesling,

French Colombard, Grey Riesling, Semillon, Barbera, Petite Sirah and Ruby Cabernet, as well as other premium grapes.

California Wine Association, Delano

This famous old company has a long history going back to 1884 when a number of California's well-known wineries, faced with a depression, joined to form the original California Wine Association.

Membership has varied over the years, but the company has always played an important part in the California wine industry. In 1929, suffering badly from Prohibition, it was reorganized as Fruit Industries Ltd., but reverted back to its former name in 1951.

For many years A. R. Morrow was the dominant figure in the association. The memory of this grand old man of California wine will always be cherished, and his name is perpetuated in one of the company's familiar brands, *A. R. Morrow* California brandy.

By 1970 the member wineries included the old Cherokee Vineyard Association at Acampo (now owned by members of the Filice family), the Rancho del Oso Winery at Lodi and A. Perelli-Minetti and Sons of Delano. In 1971 the cooperative was acquired by the latter winery and changed to a stock company headed by Antonio Perelli-Minetti, the last of the state's pre-Prohibition vintners. The winery and vineyards are now located at Delano, with the main marketing office in Burlingame near San Francisco and the eastern office in New York headed by Antonio's oldest son, Mario. Another son, William, oversees the vineyards.

Although he is on the sunny side of one hundred, Antonio Perelli-Minetti personally watches over production of CWA wines, especially the new varietals marketed under the *Ambassador* label: Chenin Blanc, Colombard, Barbera, Ruby Cabernet, Zinfandel and Petite Sirah. The 1,200 acres of family-owned vineyards also harbor a red variety developed over 50 years and patented by him, now called Perelli 101, which was to reach the market as a full-bodied table wine under the *Perelli-Minetti* label.

The son of an Italian enologist, Antonio graduated from the Royal Academy of Viticulture at Conegliano, Italy, and came to California in 1902. He made wine in Sonoma, Mendocino, Alameda and other California counties as well as Mexico before building his seventh and latest winery at Delano in 1934.

The California Wine Association is one of the largest producers in the state. It purchases varietal grapes in the Napa Valley and to a lesser extent in Sonoma County for its *Fino Eleven Cellars* table wines, crushing and fermenting them on the North Coast and then shipping the wine to Delano for aging in oak barrels.

A full line of table, aperitif, dessert and sparkling wines is produced under brands such as *Vino Fino, L & J, Greystone, Calwa, Ambassador* and *Guasti*. In addition to *A.R. Morrow* brandy, *Aristocrat* brandy is made in a unique, 50-foot column still designed by Antonio and his son, Fred, who manages the winery. The brandies are made 100% from California grapes and are aged in oak casks from 4 to 12 years before blending.

Bear Mountain Winery (M. LaMont Vineyards), DiGiorgio

This winery, successor to the DiGiorgio Wine Company, was founded in 1966, tripled in size before it finished its first decade and now ranks fourth among California's wine producers with a storage capacity approaching 30,000,000 gallons. The secret of its success lies partly in aggressive marketing, but also in the experimentation with and the propagation of high-quality grape varieties in an area that had been thought to be good only for raisins and dessert wine types.

Today the huge winery, still expanding, sits in the midst of 20,000 acres of Kern County vineyards, including nearly a quarter of the new grape acreage of California, on the rich, loamy plain that stretches up to the Tehachapi Mountains. By 1975 it was estimated that as much as 10% of California's wine grape vines were standing in this area, where 40 years ago a few thousand acres of grapes like Thompson Seedless grew.

In 1972 Bear Mountain introduced its *M. LaMont* brand of table wines, including varietals such as French Colombard, Chenin Blanc, Emerald Riesling, Semillon, Ruby Cabernet, Barbera and Zinfandel. As interesting are its three generics which, because of the great amount of premium grapes available, are actually varietal blends: the Chablis is predominantly French Colombard, the Burgundy is a Cabernet blend and the Vin Rosé is made mostly from the Grenache grape.

Giumarra Vineyards Corp., Edison

A supplier of fresh fruit from the Southern San Joaquin Valley since 1922, Joe Giumarra, with the help of his brothers, built a modern winery after World War II, and for 27 years made wine in bulk for other California vintners, eventually controlling more than 6,000 acres of vineyards. In 1974, with the rush to mid-priced varietals in America, the family introduced their own Giumarra Classic Wines.

Unlike other producers of the new valley varietals, the Giumarras vintage-date most of their wines, which were released in a unique new bottle designed especially for the company. In addition to generic Burgundy and Chablis, the line includes Chenin Blanc, French Colombard, Green Hungarian, Grenache Sec, Barbera, Zinfandel, Petite Sirah and Cabernet Rouge (Ruby Cabernet), as well as two Sherries and a Port.

Giumarra Vineyards is a family operation, with John Giumarra Sr. as executive vice president, John Jr. as general manager of wine operations and Dominick Corsaro, Joe Giumarra's brother-in-law, vice president, secretary and a director. The chief winemaker is Dale Anderson.

XIII

SOUTHERN CALIFORNIA REGION

*T*HIS, THE THIRD of the great wine producing regions of California, covers the southern part of the state, from Los Angeles and San Bernardino counties down south to the Mexican border. Its over-all climate is warm, though less hot than that of the San Joaquin Valley in the great inland valley region. It is especially noted for its dessert wines, while good table wines and champagnes of quality are also produced.

Southern California consists of a number of separate wine producing districts of which the Cucamonga district in the southwestern tip of San Bernardino County is the best known. It is followed by the city and county of Los Angeles.

There are two further districts in the region, the Riverside district in the northwest section of Riverside County adjoining Cucamonga and the Escondido district centering around the city of that name in San Diego County.

Although there are wineries in these areas dating back to the last century, such as the Rubidoux Winery in Riverside, founded in 1883, there were few vineyards or wineries of more than local importance in this century until a number of years ago, when new plantings were undertaken, especially in the Rancho California area in southwestern Riverside County north of Escondido, where 5,000 acres of new vines may have been put down by the end of the 1970s.

Here, vintners like Ely Callaway, retired president of Burlington Industries, who has been tending 100 acres, and broadcasting executive John Poole, who owns another 100 acres, are pioneering premium varietals. Callaway's winemaker, Karl Werner, made the winery's first commercial wines in 1974, with the inevitable consultation of Andre Tchelistcheff.

They have joined a number of vintners who have kept the faith in Southern California in the face of smog and the creeping megalopolis: the Louis Cherpin Winery at Fontana since 1934, J. Filippi Vintage Co. founded at Mira Loma the same year, the neighboring Galleano Winery established in 1948 and the quarter-century-old Aggazzotti Winery at Cucamonga.

According to tradition it was in San Diego County that Padre Junipero Serra planted the first wine grapes in 1769.

A. *CUCAMONGA DISTRICT*

Cucamonga, one of the few places in California to retain its old Indian name, is said to be derived from "Cucamongabit," meaning "Land of Many Springs." Cucamonga Indians were living in the district when the Spaniards came and built their El Camino Real. In 1839 Don Tiburcio Tapia, who became president of the Ayuntamiento, or City Council, of Los Angeles and the city's first *alcalde,* obtained the Cucamonga grant from the Mexican Government. It is known that Don Tapia also planted grape vines on the ranch.

Cucamonga was the scene of many turbulent events in its early days and its history makes fascinating reading. Gradually it passed from the violent and romantic Wild West stages to an equally romantic but more peaceful era of agriculture and industry. Magnificently situated in the San Bernardino Valley in the extreme southwestern corner of the county of that name, it lies at the foot of the grandiose

range of the San Gabriel Mountains with Cucamonga Peak dominating the scene from an altitude of some 8000 feet.

The Cucamonga wine growing district has become increasingly
famous over the years. It centers around the town of Cucamonga,
straddling Highways 66 and 99 and spreading north to Etiwanda
and Alta Loma and south to Ontario, Guasti, and the Riverside
County line. It is threatened, however, like many other wine growing areas, by the encroachment of real estate developments.

The Cucamonga district is noted for its red table wines, especially
Barbera, Grignolino, Zinfandel, and Chianti. These should be consumed young, as they mature early, owing to the warm climate in
which the grapes are grown. New plantings of white varieties such
as Emerald Riesling and even Chardonnay have been undertaken.
Cucamonga is also well known for its champagnes and aperitif and
dessert wines, including ports, sherries, and vermouths.

Cucamonga Vineyard Company, Cucamonga

The enterprise, formerly the Padre Vineyard Company, is now
known as the Cucamonga Vineyard Company. The winery, founded
in 1870, was rebuilt by the Vai family in 1909 and enjoys the distinction of being California's Bonded Winery No. 1.

Mrs. James L. Vai, who succeeded her husband, and her son,
Cesare Vai, sold the winery in 1972 to Pacific American Industries
Inc. Manuel Yellen is president, and Cesare Vai remained as a
vice president.

Prior to the acquisition, the winery concentrated on custom
bottlings of table and sparkling wines for restaurants and clubs, but
under the new management, both entered national distribtuion
under the brands *Pierre Monté, Don Brut, California Bonded
Winery No. 1* and *Cesare.* The Vais' *San Gabriel* brand, which
once was marketed by the famous old San Gabriel Winery, was
discontinued.

Assumption Abbey Winery

(see **Brookside Vineyard Company,** below)

Brookside Vineyard Company, Guasti

The owners of this historic family enterprise are the Bianes, wine growers and wine makers in the district for five generations. Philo Biane, the president of the firm, has been in the wine business of the region continuously for over sixty years.

The firm was originally founded by Théophile Vaché who came from his native island of Oléron in France by way of Cape Horn to California in 1830. Two years later he is said to have engaged in the wine business in Monterey, then still under the Mexican flag. He certainly was one of the pioneers of the California wine industry as in 1849 or even earlier he planted vines south of Hollister in San Benito County in the so-called "Vineyard District" later to become the Valliant Vineyards, now leased by Almadén (see there).

Three nephews of Théophile Vaché the elder came to California to join their uncle: Émile, Théophile the younger and Adolphe. A fourth brother, Alfred, remained in France to operate the family winery and distillery. Émile later returned to his native country as did Théophile the elder but Théophile the younger and Adolphe remained in California. Eventually the family moved to Southern California founding a wholesale business of fine wines and spirits in the heart of downtown Los Angeles. In 1882 the Vaché brothers established themselves as "Wholesale Dealers and Rectifiers and Manufacturers of Native Wines, Brandies, Wine Vinegar, Syrups, Etc.," at Old San Bernardino, leasing the winery which Dr. Benjamin Barton had built some years before. The next year they moved to Redlands Junction, hardly a town at that time, some ten miles southeast of San Bernardino, where they built the Brookside Winery.

A French lad by the name of Marius Biane arrived in 1892 from his native district of Gers in Gascony and soon went to work for the brothers Vaché at Brookside. He fell in love with Marcelline,

Adolphe Vaché's daughter, and married her. In due course the Biane family carried on the Vaché tradition of wine making in Redlands, Marius also acquiring vineyards in the Cucamonga district. In 1916 the winery was sold and Marius Biane's sons, Philo and François, went to work for Garrett & Company and later for Fruit Industries Ltd., as the California Wine Association (see there) was known at one time. It was not till 1952 that the Bianes revived their own enterprise by re-establishing the Brookside Vineyard Company at Ontario, moving in 1956 to Guasti at their present location.

The Guasti plant which the Bianes purchased from the California Wine Association, built in 1904, has vast storage cellars with walls of stone, three feet thick. One of the units has an underground space, 20 feet below the surface, 175 feet long by 100 feet wide, used for the storage and aging of wines prior to shipment.

Marius Biane has since died. His son, Philo, is president and general manager. The fifth generation of the wine making family is represented by Philo's sons, Michael and Pierre, and by René, the son of François (Frank) Biane who passed away in 1958.

The featured brand for premium wines is *Brookside* and under this label generic table wines and Zinfandel as well as aperitif and dessert wines including dry and sweet vermouth are available. *E. Vaché* is a subsidiary brand.

The Brookside Winery has for long been noted for its Altar Wines and in its expansion and promotion of the finer wines was approached by the Benedictine Monks of Assumption Abbey, Richardton, North Dakota, to enter into working arrangements with them whereby it would be possible to start the Benedictines in the wine business in the New World, following their ancient Old World tradition.

This was accomplished and so the Assumption Abbey Winery was formed as a D.B.A.* of Brookside Vineyards Company and the *Assumption Abbey* brand was launched.

* Doing Business As.

The Benedictine Monks, one of the oldest orders of the Roman Catholic Church, have been characterized by lives devoted to prayer, study and labor. Though devotion is primary, they exemplify Saint Benedict's Rule that monks "live by the work of their hands." Their 1400 year background in the production of wines and related beverages is known the world over. The wonder and skill of the Benedictines' art in wine making and to uplift the heart of man is now captured in Assumption Abbey wines, carrying on the world respected and centuries old Benedictine tradition.

Abbot Hunkler, who was the Abbot of Assumption Abbey when the project began, was known throughout the Benedictine communities as the "Wine Abbot." He has been replaced by Abbot Robert West, and the Abbey's wines, produced by the Bianes at their Brookside Winery in Guasti, enjoy a national distribution, from New York to California and from Louisiana to Minnesota.

The wines sold to the public include Petite Sirah, Cabernet, Dido Noir and Zinfandel in the reds; Pinot Chardonnay, Johannisberg Riesling, Chenin Blanc, Emerald Riesling, St. Emilion and Vertdoux Blanc in the whites, and Vin Rosé. Aperitif and dessert wines are Tinta Port, Sherry Palido, Sherry De Oro, Sherry Crema, Cream Marsala and Cream Muscat.

Assumption Abbey Altar wines are available to the clergy under the same brand. In addition to the still wines mentioned above, there are two bottle-fermented champagnes, *Brut* and Extra Dry, and an aged brandy.

In 1969 Brookside acquired the 12 Mills Winery roadside cellars in Northern California, making the company, with 16 cellars of its own already in the south, the largest direct-to-the-consumer winery operation in the country.

Brookside also has started new vineyards in the Rancho California agricultural complex at Temecula, an area designated by University of California scientists as Regions II and III, similar to the Napa and Sonoma valleys. The company has 1,000 acres under its control, and plans call for 5,000 acres eventually. The first varietals

from the new vines, Petite Sirah, Emerald Riesling and Johannisberg Riesling, were on the market in 1971.

Five years later, as the Rancho California vineyards matured,
Pinot Chardonnay, Gamay Beaujolais, Pinot Noir and Cabernet
Sauvignon from Temecula were added to the list.

B. *THE CITY AND COUNTY OF LOS ANGELES*

Where some 20 years ago Los Angeles still counted twelve wineries, this number has now decreased to a few wineries and bonded cellars. No more, alas, is the old San Gabriel Winery in operation at
San Gabriel. The time when Los Angeles led California in wine
growing and wine production has long since passed. Real estate developments, freeways and other changes of the times, such is the
price one has to pay for progress. Often willingly, let it be said.
Where Anaheim once was a German colony devoted to the growing
of wines, it is now the home of Disneyland.

Navé Pierson Winery, Los Angeles

The first new winery to be established in Los Angeles since 1917
was founded in 1970 by Les Navé, a rocket test engineer from Hollywood, and Sam Pierson, a former professional photographer, of
South Pasadena.

Within five years the winery was producing 100,000 gallons a
year of table, dessert, sparkling and fruit wines. In addition to the
tasting room on San Fernando Road in the city's industrial area, a
second has been opened in Palm Springs. Sam Pierson has long
since become a full-time winemaker, and now is chairman, president
and general manager.

On weekends the winery features jazz concerts on the patio,
which have become increasingly popular.

San Antonio Winery, Los Angeles

While Navé Pierson is the newest winery in Los Angeles, San Antonio is the oldest still in operation, having been founded in 1917 by Santo Cambianica, who came to America from northern Italy with his three brothers and went to work for the Southern Pacific Railroad. His first winery building was constructed from the sturdy siding of old freight cars.

Santo's nephew, Steve Riboli, the present owner, was born two blocks from the winery, but was sent to school in Italy and didn't return until after Prohibition, which the business had survived by making sacramental and medicinal wines. Members of the family, including Steve's son, Santo, the vice president, still have the habit of working seven days a week, picked up during the lean years of the Depression. The winery has prospered, although as recently as 1966 it was threatened with condemnation so that a public transportation center could be built. Today the winery, about five blocks off the Santa Ana Freeway near the rail yards, is designated as a historic-cultural landmark by the city, and has been cited for beautifying the neighborhood and building a small park.

San Antonio Winery buys its grapes from the Riverside, Lodi and Rancho California areas, and also buys wine which is aged, blended and bottled under its label. A good deal of the wines are sold through eight company-owned tasting rooms, some of which have cafes attached.

In addition to the regular line of table and fortified wines, the Ribolis are very proud of their sweet, specialty wines such as Marsalovo (a Marsala with egg and spices) and Almondoro (flavored with almonds).

With a final tribute to the memory of Jean Louis Vignes and his famed Aliso Vineyard that once covered over a hundred acres of what is now the heart of downtown Los Angeles and with a bow to the Mission Fathers headed by Fra Junipero Serra who were the first to plant and cultivate grapes along the shores of the Pacific, Part Two of this *Guide* comes to a somewhat reluctant close.

Part Three

XIV

HANDY WINE AND FOOD GUIDE

*W*HAT WINE to serve with a particular dish or at a special occasion? At what temperature will a wine taste the best and give the most value for the money? This and related information is presented in charts in the following pages.

The how and when of serving wines has been overdone. It has also been underdone. Wines *are* at their best at certain temperatures. Certain wines *do* go better with certain foods. There is no point in denying the facts. After all, coffee tastes better hot than tepid and orange juice is tastiest when cold. The same with wines. Red table wines will give the greatest enjoyment when served at the temperature of the room and white table wines when they are chilled. Lukewarm champagne is to no one's liking and overicing it will kill its natural flavor and bouquet. Stirring champagne with a swizzle stick is idiotic, killing the very bubbles it has cost a fortune and centuries of experience to create. So it is really only sage to observe certain very simple rules.

Suggestions follow for nearly every occasion. Should you not agree with them, you can always suit yourself.

194

A. *WINE WITH, BEFORE AND AFTER MEALS*

Eleven O'Clock (Elevenses)

with English biscuits or cookies.....Sherry (dry or medium), *Brut* or *Extra Dry* Champagne

Lunch

before lunch.....................Sherry (dry or medium), *Brut* Champagne

with lunch.......................Grenache Rosé, Gamay Rosé or other Rosé; *White table wine:* Semillon (dry or medium), Sauvignon Blanc (dry or medium), Chardonnay, Pinot Blanc, Chenin Blanc, Folle Blanche, White (Johannisberg) Riesling, Traminer, Sylvaner, Grey Riesling

with picnic lunch.................Grenache Rosé, Gamay Rosé or other Rosé

Afternoon Refreshments

with cookies or cake..............Port, Muscat, Sherry (medium or sweet); *Extra dry* or *Demi Sec* Champagne; Grenache Rosé, Gamay Rosé or other Rosé

Cocktail Party (6–8 o'clock)

with canapes.....................*Brut* or *Extra Dry* Champagne, Sherry (dry, medium or sweet), Port, Muscat, Sweet Vermouth

Cocktail Party (6–10 o'clock or later)

with ham, turkey, cold cuts or
casserole dinner................*Brut* or *Extra Dry* Champagne;
Cabernet Sauvignon, Pinot Noir or
Gamay; Grenache Rosé, Gamay Rosé
or other Rosé

Dinner

before dinner....................*Brut* or *Extra Dry* Champagne; Dry
Sherry or Dry Port

with dinner (one wine, white or
red, depending on the main
course, see B. Specific Dishes)..RED: Cabernet Sauvignon, Pinot
Noir, Gamay, Zinfandel, Barbera,
Grignolino
WHITE: Semillon (dry or medium),
Sauvignon Blanc (dry or medium),
Chardonnay, Pinot Blanc, Pinot
Blanc de Noir, Chenin Blanc, White
(Johannisberg) Riesling, Traminer
or Gewurztraminer, Sylvaner, Grey
Riesling

with dinner (one wine regardless
of dish).......................*Extra Dry* Champagne throughout
with formal dinner (two entrees)...If white and red, first the white, then
the red; if two reds, Cabernet Sau-
vignon followed by Pinot Noir

with dinner (one table wine and
one with the dessert)..........Red or white table wine with the
main course
With the dessert: Sweet Semillon,
Sweet Sauvignon Blanc, Chateau
Sauterne, *Demi Sec* or *Sec* Cham-

pagne, Moscato Amabile, Moscato
Spumante, Port, Muscat

after dinner......................Brandy

Supper (after the theatre)

regardless ....*Brut* or *Extra Dry* Champagne

Nightcap

with a snack....................A split (¼ bottle) of *Extra Dry* or
Demi Sec Champagne, Port, Muscat,
Sweet Sherry

At Any Time of Day or Night

with English biscuits or cookies....*Brut* or *Extra Dry* Champagne

B. *WINE WITH SPECIFIC DISHES*

THE DISH	THE SUGGESTIONS

Before the Meal

Canapes or Hors d'Oeuvres........*Brut* or *Extra Dry* Champagne, Dry
Sherry

Caviar or Lumpfish..............*Brut* Champagne

Oysters, Fish and Shellfish

Oysters or Clams.................Chardonnay, Pinot Blanc, White
(Johannisberg) Riesling, Traminer,
Sylvaner, Grey Riesling; *Brut* or
Extra Dry Champagne

Fish or Shellfish, plain (boiled,
broiled, poached)..............Semillon (dry or medium), Sauvi-

gnon Blanc (dry or medium), Chardonnay, Pinot Blanc, Chenin Blanc (dry), Folle Blanche, White (Johannisberg) Riesling, Traminer, Sylvaner, Grey Riesling, Green Hungarian

Fish or Shellfish, creamed.........Semillon (medium or sweet), Sauvignon Blanc (medium or sweet), Chenin Blanc (sweet)

Soups

Clear Soup......................Dry Sherry
Creamed Soup...................Medium Dry Sherry

Eggs and Salads

Eggs of any kind................No wine as eggs and wine don't mix
Salads ....No wine as it does not blend with vinegar or lemon

White Meat

Veal, Pork.....................Semillon (medium), Sauvignon Blanc (medium), Chenin Blanc (medium); Gamay, Zinfandel; Grenache Rosé, Gamay Rosé or other Rosé

Red Meat

Tournedos, Chateaubriand, Filet
  Mignon, Steak, Roast Beef......Cabernet Sauvignon
Pot Roast, Stew, Spareribs, Short
  Ribs, Meat Patties.............Gamay, Zinfandel
Beef Burgundy..................Pinot Noir
Steak and Kidney Pie...........Cabernet Sauvignon, Zinfandel

Beef Stroganoff...................Gamay, Zinfandel
Lamb...........................Zinfandel, Gamay

Ham

Hot or Cold....................Semillon (medium), Sauvignon
Blanc (medium), Pinot Blanc, Pinot
Blanc de Noir; Grenache Rosé,
Gamay Rosé or other Rosé

Poultry

Chicken (broiled, roasted, fried,
stewed).......................Red or white table wine.
RED: Cabernet Sauvignon, Zinfandel,
Gamay, Pinot Noir. For *white* table
wine choice see Fish or Shellfish,
plain

Chicken, creamed...............White table wine; for choice see Fish
or Shellfish, creamed

Turkey, roasted.................Red or white table wine, red pre-
ferred, see Chicken, broiled
On festive occasions: *Extra Dry*
Champagne or Sparkling Burgundy

Long Island Duckling, Goose......Cabernet Sauvignon, Gamay, Zinfandel, Pinot Noir

Game

Wild Duck, Partridge, Pheasant,
Quail, Squab, Venison..........Cabernet Sauvignon, Gamay, Pinot
Noir

Rabbit

Tame or Wild...................Cabernet Sauvignon, Gamay, Zinfandel, Pinot Noir

Variety Meats and Frogs' Legs

Sweetbreads, Brains, Frogs' Legs...Semillon (medium or sweet), Sau-
vignon Blanc (medium or sweet),
Chenin Blanc (medium or sweet),
Traminer or Gewurztraminer

Kidneys, Heart, Tripe, Liver......Zinfandel, Gamay

Cold Cuts

At lunch, dinner or supper........Grenache Rosé, Gamay Rosé or other
Rosé; Semillon (dry), Sauvignon
Blanc (dry); Chardonnay, Pinot
Blanc, Chenin Blanc (dry), Folle
Blanche; White (Johannisberg) Ries-
ling, Traminer, Sylvaner, Grey Ries-
ling, Green Hungarian; Zinfandel,
Gamay

Casseroles

Any of these.....................Red or white table wine depending
on what the casserole is made of

Foreign and Exotic Dishes

Spaghetti, Macaroni, Pizza and
  other Italian Dishes (Pastas)....Barbera,   Grignolino,   Charbono,
Chianti
Goulash ....Zinfandel
Mexican Dishes..................Lager, Ale or Beer
Curried Dishes..................Lager, Ale or Beer
Indonesian Rijsttafel.............Lager, Ale or Beer
Highly Seasoned Dishes..........Lager, Ale or Beer

Cheese

Assorted Cheeses.................Cabernet Sauvignon, Pinot Noir, Port

Welsh Rarebit...................Lager, Ale or Beer

Dessert

Desserts, Fruit and Nuts..........Semillon (sweet), Sauvignon Blanc (sweet), Chateau (type) Sauternes, Chenin Blanc (sweet), *Demi Sec* or *Sec* Champagne, Moscato Amabile, Moscato Spumante, Port, Muscat.

C. *SPECIAL OCCASIONS*

Wedding Receptions..............*Brut* or *Extra Dry* Champagne
Christening Receptions...........*Brut* or *Extra Dry* Champagne
Birthdays and other anniversaries,
    men ....*Brut* Champagne
Birthdays and other anniversaries,
    women ....*Extra Dry* Champagne, Pink Champagne (Rosé)
New Year's Eve..................*Extra Dry* Champagne
As a gift for any occasion.........A bottle or case of any fine wine
Thanksgiving or Christmas Dinner.Cabernet Sauvignon, Pinot Noir, *Extra Dry* Champagne, Sparkling Burgundy or Champagne Rouge.

D. *GENERAL SUGGESTIONS*

Storage of Wines

The best place...................Cellar or closet
The temperature.................About fifty-five degrees

The position.....................Lying down to keep the cork moist
The manner.....................Bins or shelves or wooden cases or cartons stood on edge; diamond shaped bins are the best but simple cartons with dividers will do very nicely.

Serving of Wines

White table wines................Cold, as they taste better that way, the sweeter the wine, the colder, but they lose their flavor when over-iced. Two to four hours in the refrigerator is about right.

Red table wines.................At the temperature of the room

Sparkling wines.................Cold, but not too cold. Two to four hours in the refrigerator is about right.

Rosé table wines................Same as white table wines (see above)

Sherry, Port, Muscat.............Same as red table wines (see above)

Should the bottle be opened before
serving? ....Yes, to let the wine "breathe" and release its bouquet; open white wines one half hour, red wines an hour before serving

When should a wine be decanted?..In the case of fine table wines and Port wines that have thrown a deposit

What is the best wine to use in
cooking?......................The best and finest only, as they have the most character and flavor; in the case of table wines use the same wine for cooking as served at table with the dish

Who is served first?..............The host always, who pours a small amount in his glass to make certain the wine tastes right

Serving white California table
wine:........................Semillon or Sauvignon Blanc; Chardonnay, Pinot Blanc, Pinot Blanc de
Noir, Chenin Blanc, Folle Blanche;
White (Johannisberg) Riesling, Traminer or Gewurztraminer, Sylvaner,
Grey Riesling

Serving red California table wines:..Cabernet Sauvignon, Zinfandel;
Pinot Noir, Gamay; Barbera, Gri-
gnolino, Charbono

Serving rosé California table wines:.Grenache Rosé, Gamay Rosé, Cabernet Rosé, Zinfandel Rosé, Grignolino
Rosé

Serving California Champagne:....*Brut* before the meal, *Extra Dry* during and *Demi Sec* or *Sec* with the
dessert; Pink Champagne for the
ladies

Serving California Sherry:.........*flor* or non-*flor Sherry,* but made
from the Palomino grape

Serving California Port:...........Tinta (Madeira) Port preferably

Serving California Muscat:........Muscat Frontignan (white) or Black
Muscat (red).

Note: Preference has been given here, as elsewhere in this *Guide,* to
the *varietal* wines as in general they will have the most character, bouquet
and flavor. They are also, both as far as character and as name are concerned, typically and distinctively Californian.

XV

MODERN WINE GLASSES

*T*HERE WAS A TIME, not long ago, when decent American wine glasses were hard to obtain. Americans, so generous in most other instances and inclined to like everything big and large and vast, clung for some unexplained reason to puny wine glasses that could do honor to no wine, let alone the host or hostess. They still cling to them, especially in the restaurants where a proper, generous sized wine glass is a rare thing to behold. Recently, thank goodness, American glass manufacturers have seen the light and fair sized wine glasses are available for the home to those who want them.

Modern usage, led by the French firm of Baccarat, the leader in wine glass ware for some centuries, demands wine glasses that are simple, pleasing, elegant in design and that hold about *twice as much wine as one is likely to serve in them*. They should be clear, easy to hold and without gingerbread.

In general the tulip or bowl shaped glasses are considered the most satisfactory. Their stems should be thin, but not too thin; they should above all hold enough to allow the wine to breathe and to release its bouquet. They should never be hollow stemmed as this makes it difficult to clean them adequately. They should be things of joy to own, to look at with pleasure. They should grace the table and shine or sparkle. They should never be small or puny.

A number of acceptable designs for wine glasses will be found on the following pages. They are suggestions only, adaptable to variations.

1. All purpose table wine
8 ounces

2. Claret or Burgundy
10 ounces

3. White wine
6 ounces

4. Rhine wine
6 ounces

1. All purpose table wine glass

Tulip shaped wine glass suited for any table wine, red, white or rosé, holding 8 ounces. A good all purpose type wine glass so that, owning no other wine glass, one still can be correctly prepared for any occasion.

2. Claret or Burgundy glass

Large tulip shaped wine glass, specially suited for a fine Cabernet Sauvignon or Pinot Noir or for any fine Claret or Red Burgundy. It holds 10 ounces but 12 ounces is also appropriate.

3. White table wine glass

Bowl or tangerine shaped wine glass designed for California white wines such as Semillon and Sauvignon Blanc; Chardonnay, Pinot Blanc, Pinot Blanc de Noir, Chenin Blanc or for any wine of the Sauternes, Graves, Chablis and White Burgundy families. It holds 6 ounces and can also be used at a dessert wine glass of Sweet Semillon, Sweet Sauvignon Blanc or Sweet Sauternes.

4. Rhine wine glass

Tall, curved bowl shaped wine glass specifically suited for any white wine of the rhine wine order such as White or Johannisberg Riesling, Traminer or Gewurztraminer, Sylvaner and Grey Riesling or for any wine, of course, of the Rhine and Moselle families. Contents 6 ounces.

Formerly such rhine wine glasses were green, amber or even rose in color; modern practice requires them to be crystal white.

5. Tulip Champagne glass

Tall tulip shaped champagne glass, holding 10 ounces and conforming to modern good taste. It is an elegant type glass, which has supplanted both the flute shaped champagne glass and the familiar saucer shaped champagne glass that is still to be found in many homes and in most restaurants and nightclubs.

5. *Tulip Champagne*
10 ounces

6. *Port or Muscat*
4–5 ounces

7. *Sherry or Aperitif*
4–5 ounces

The saucer champagne glass will be with us for years to come as it has become so strongly identified with the serving of champagne or any other sparkling wine. Yet the tall tulip shaped champagne glass is much more elegant, distinctive and better suited for the purpose. It should, of course, never be hollow stemmed (see introduction to this chapter).

6. Port or Muscat glass

This is a typical modern and pleasing dessert wine glass, suited well for Port, Muscat or for any other dessert wine, served either with the dessert or between meals with light refreshments. It holds 4 to 5 ounces and, like any other wine glass, should be about half filled.

7. Sherry or Aperitif glass

Contrary to popular belief, the best Sherry glasses are not the traditional V-shaped vessels which look as if they should hold Martinis, although they are the ones most often sold. Preferable are "chimney" glasses holding 4–6 ounces, capable of capturing and accentuating the aroma and bouquet of the wine.

XVI

A LIST OF OUTSTANDING
CALIFORNIA WINES

*T*HIS LIST is arranged alphabetically according to wine type. Preference has been given to the varietal wines as they are more typically Californian both in character and name.

While most of the wines named are vintage dated, some are blends of various years. We have refrained from commenting on the differences between vintages (and notwithstanding industry statements to the contrary, there ARE differences between vintages in California) because, with only a few exceptions, California vintage wines are released and sold young, and those of particular years become unavailable rapidly. Therefore, these wineries were selected for fairly consistent quality instead of momentary greatness.

The list reflects several years worth of impressions and notes from tastings large and small, public and private, and, of course, the prejudices of the author. It is intended only as a very general guide. In every case there is a description of the winery earlier in the book.

A. CALIFORNIA RED TABLE WINES

Cabernet Sauvignon (the premier claret type wine of California)
Beaulieu	Freemark Abbey
Davis Bynum	Heitz
Concannon	Ingelnook

Charles Krug   Robert Mondavi
Llords & Elwood   Nicasio Vineyards
Oakville   Sebastiani
Louis Martini   Souverain
Mayacamas   Spring Mountain
Mirassou   Stag's Leap Wine Cellars

Zinfandel (typical California red table wine of better than average quality, fruity and zestful)

Buena Vista   Mayacamas
Davis Bynum   Mirassou
Conradi   Oakville
D'Agostini   Parducci
Foppiano   Pedroncelli
Fetzer   Ridge
Grand Cru   Souverain
Heitz   Trentadue
Charles Krug   Conrad Viano
Louis Martini   York Mountain

Pinot Noir (the great red burgundy type wine)

Beaulieu   Inglenook
Davis Bynum   Llords & Elwood
Chalone   Louis Martini
Freemark Abbey   Robert Mondavi
Hanzell   Mirassou
Heitz   Weibel
Husch

Gamay (the Beaujolais type wine)

Beaulieu   Mirassou
Christian Brothers   Robert Mondavi
Charles Krug   Sebastiani
Oakville   Wente Brothers
Paul Masson

Barbera (full flavored Italian type wine)

Cresta Blanca	Louis Martini
E. & J. Gallo	Rapazzini
Heitz	Sebastiani

Grignolino (light colored red wine of Italian origin, see also Grignolino Rosé)

Cadenasso	Heitz
Cresta Blanca	San Martin

Charbono (soft Italian type red table wine of Piedmontese origin)
Inglenook

Petite Sirah (the grape of France's Rhône Valley)

Concannon	Mirassou
Cresta Blanca	Sonoma Vineyards
Freemark Abbey	Wente Brothers

B. CALIFORNIA WHITE TABLE WINES

Sauvignon Blanc (the more aromatic of the Sauternes type wines)

Almadén (Blanc Fumé)	Oakville
Beaulieu	Roudon-Smith
Concannon	Spring Mountain
Charles Krug	Wente Brothers
Robert Mondavi (Fumé Blanc)	

Semillon (fruity and flavorful wine of the Sauternes type)

Concannon	Louis Martini
Inglenook	San Martin
Charles Krug	Wente Brothers
Paul Masson (Chateau Masson)	

Chardonnay (the Chablis and White Burgundy-type wine)

Beaulieu	Mayacamas
Buena Vista	Mirassou
Burgess Cellars	Robert Mondavi
Chalone	Nicasio Vineyards
Chappellet	Sonoma Vineyards
Freemark Abbey	Souverain
Hanzell	Spring Mountain
Heitz	Stony Hill
Charles Krug	Wente Brothers

Pinot Blanc (White Burgundy type wine from the Pinot blanc grape)

Chalone	Mirassou
Heitz	Wente Brothers

Chenin Blanc (Vouvray type wine from Chenin blanc or Pineau de la Loire grapes)

Beringer	Charles Krug
Burgess	Louis Martini
Chalone	Mirassou
Christian Brothers	Oakville
Inglenook	Woodside Vineyards

Folle Blanche (from that grape, a fresh, light luncheon wine)

Louis Martini

White Riesling or *Johannisberg Riesling* (the premier California wine of the Rhine wine order)

Almadén	Louis Martini
Beaulieu	Robert Mondavi
Beringer	Chateau Montelena
Concannon	Nicasio Vineyards
Freemark Abbey	Sebastiani
Heitz	Souverain
Charles Krug	Stag's Leap Wine Cellars
Llords & Elwood	Veedercrest

Traminer and *Gewurztraminer* (aromatic wine of the Alsatian type from
the Traminer grape)

Hacienda	Loius Martini
Husch	Mirassou
Charles Krug	Robert Mondavi

Grey Riesling (light wine from Grey Riesling or Chauché gris grapes)

Beringer	Weibel
Charles Krug	Wente Brothers

C. CALIFORNIA ROSÉ TABLE WINES

Grenache Rosé (from Grenache grapes)

Almadén	Weibel
Beaulieu	

Gamay Rosé (from Gamay grapes)

Butte Creek	Robert Mondavi
Louis Martini	Oakville

Cabernet Rosé (from Cabernet Sauvignon grapes)

Buena Vista	Llord & Elwood
Davis Bynum	Simi

Zinfandel Rosé (from Zinfandel grapes)

Concannon	Pedroncelli
Nichelini	Conrad Viano

Grignolino Rosé (see also under Grignolino)

Heitz

D. CALIFORNIA CHAMPAGNE

Champagne
  Almadén *Blanc de Blancs*
  Beaulieu Private Reserve *Brut*
  Korbel *Natural* and *Brut*
  Hanns Kornell *Sehr Trocken,*
    Brut and *Extra Dry*
  Llords & Elwood *Extra Dry*

  Mirassou *Au Natural* and *Brut*
  Schramsberg *Blanc de Blancs*
    and *Blanc de Noir*
  Weibel *Chardonnay Brut*
  Windsor *Brut*

Pink (Rosé) Champagne
  Christian Brothers
  Korbel
  Hanns Kornell

  Paul Masson
  Schramsberg *Cuvée de Gamay*
  Weibel

Red Champagne (Sparkling Burgundy)
  Almadén
  Korbel
  Hanns Kornell
  Paul Masson

  Mirassou *Sparkling Gamay*
    Beaujolais
  Weibel

Moscato Amabile (slightly effervescent Muscat)
  Bargetto

  Louis Martini

E. CALIFORNIA APERITIF and DESSERT WINES

Sherry (Dry, Medium and Sweet)
  Buena Vista
  Davis Bynum

  Cresta Blanca
  Hacienda

Llords & Elwood   Richert & Sons
Louis Martini

Port (Ruby, Tawny and Vintage)
Buena Vista   Llords & Elwood
Ficklin   Paul Masson

Muscat de Frontignan
Concannon Muscat de Frontignan
Novitiate of Los Gatos Muscat Frontignan

Black Muscat
Novitiate of Los Gatos Black Muscat
Weibel Cream of Black Muscat

WINE MAP OF California

SONOMA-MENDOCINO

NAPA VALLEY-SOLANO

ALAMEDA-CONTRA COSTA

SANTA CLARA-SAN BENITO-SANTA CRUZ

LODI-SACRAMENTO

ESCALON-MODESTO

FRESNO-SAN JOAQUIN VALLEY

SOUTHERN CALIFORNIA

XVII

A LIST OF CALIFORNIA WINERIES OPEN TO THE PUBLIC

(This list is of main wineries only, and does not include a great many winery-owned tasting rooms. In addition, many wineries not open to the public and not listed here welcome visitors by appointment. For periodically updated information write for the *California's Wine Wonderland* booklet from the Wine Institute, 165 Post St., San Francisco, California 94108.)

Alameda County

ALBANY
   Bynum Winery
   614 San Pablo Avenue
   526-1366

LIVERMORE
   Concannon Vineyard
   P. O. Box 432
   HIlltop 7-3760

   Wente Bros.
   5565 Tesla Road
   HIlltop 7-3603

MISSION SAN JOSE
   Weibel Champagne Vineyards
   P. O. Box 3095
   OLiver 6-9914

OAKLAND
   Veedercrest Vineyards*
   6823 Buckingham
   652-0186

PLEASANTON
   Villa Armando Winery
   124 St. Johns Street
   VIctor 6-1451

   Ruby Hill Vineyard Co.
   1188 Vineyard Avenue
   846-2004

* By appointment only.

217

Amador County

PLYMOUTH
D'Agostini Winery
Box 66, Aukum Road
CHapel 5-6612

Contra Costa County

MARTINEZ
J. E. Digardi   Conrad Viano Winery
P. O. Box 88   Morello Road
ACademy 8-2638   228-6465

El Dorado County

COLOMA
Coloma Wine Cellars   Gold Hill Winery
P. O. Box 270   P. O. Box 267
622-2275   622-1712

Fresno County

FRESNO   PARLIER (contd.)
Antonio Nonini Winery   Nicholas G. Verry Inc.
2640 N. Dickenson Avenue   400 First Street
AMherst 4-7857   646-2785

Roma Wine Company   SANGER
3223 E. Church Avenue   Sanger Winery Association
485-8581   1720 Academy Avenue
                                        TRinity 5-2505
PARLIER
Christian Bros.
(Mt. Tivy Winery)
8418 S. Lac Jac
638-3544

Kern County

DELANO
California Wine Association
Pond Road
792-3162

DIGIORGIO
Bear Mountain Winery
Winery Road
845-2231

EDISON
Giumarra Vineyards
Corporation
P. O. Box 98
366-7251

Los Angeles County

LOS ANGELES
Nave Pierson Winery
1204 San Fernando Rd.
221-0167

San Antonio Winery, Inc.
737 Lamar Street
223-1401

Madera County

MADERA
Bisceglia Bros. Wine Company
Highway 99
674-2545

Ficklin Vineyards*
30246 Avenue 7½
674-4598

Mendocino County

PHILO
Edmeades Vineyards
Highway 128
895-3232

Husch Vineyards*
Highway 128

REDWOOD VALLEY
Fetzer Vineyards*
Bel Arbres Road
485-8998

UKIAH
Cresta Blanca
Lake Mendocino Drive
462-5161

Parducci Wine Cellars
Parducci Road
462-3828

Weibel Champagne Vineyards
7051 N. State Street
485-0321

* By appointment only.

Napa County

CALISTOGA
  Schramsberg Vineyards*
  WHitehall 2-4558

  Sterling Vineyards
  Dunaweal Lane
  942-5151

NAPA
  Mayacamas Vineyards*
  1155 Lokoya Road

  Mont La Salle Vineyards
  P. O. Box 420
  BAldwin 6-5566

OAKVILLE
  Oakville Vineyards
  P. O. Box 87
  944-2455

  Robert Mondavi Winery
  P. O. Box 403
  963-7156

RUTHERFORD
  Beaulieu Vineyard
  WOodward 3-3671

  Inglenook Vineyard Company
  WOodward 3-7184

  Souverain
  Souverain Road
  963-2750

ST. HELENA
  Beringer Bros.
  2000 Main Street
  WOodward 3-7115

  Burgess Cellars
  1108 Deer Park Rd.
  963-4766

  Chappellet Winery*
  1581 Sage Road
  963-7136

  Conradi Vineyard*
  Spring Mountain Road
  963-7511

  Freemark Abbey
  WOodward 3-7106

  Heitz Wine Cellars
  436 St. Helena Highway S.
  963-3542

  Hanns Kornell Cellars
  Larkmead Lane
  WOodward 3-2334

  Charles Krug Winery
    (C. Mondavi and Sons)
  P. O. Box 191
  WOodward 3-2761

  Louis M. Martini
  P. O. Box 112
  WOodward 3-2736

* By appointment only.

Napa County (contd.)

St. Helena (contd.)
 Nichelini Vineyard
 State Highway 128
 963-3357

 Spring Mountain Vineyards*
 Spring Mountain Road
 963-4341

Sutter Home Winery
 State Highway 29
 WOodward 3-3104

Sacramento County

Elk Grove
 Gibson Wine Company
 P. O. Drawer E
 MUrray 5-9594

Florin
 James Frasinetti & Sons
 First Street
 383-2444

San Bernadino County

Alta Loma
 Opici Winery Inc.
 P. O. Box 56
 YUkon 7-2710

Cucamonga
 Aggazzotti Winery
 11929 Foothill Boulevard
 YUkon 7-1657

 Thomas Vineyards
 8916 Foothill Boulevard
 YUkon 7-1612

Fontana
 Louis Cherpin
 15567 Valley Boulevard
  (U.S. 99)
 VAlley 2-4103

 J. Filippi Vintage Co.
 Etiwanda Avenue
 984-4514

Guasti
 Brookside Vineyard Company
  (Assumption Abbey Winery)
 9900 A Street
 986-9377

* By appointment only.

San Diego County

ESCONDIDO
Ferrara Winery
1120 West 15th Street
SHerwood 5-7632

San Joaquin County

ACAMPO
Barengo Cellars
East End Orange Street
ENdicott 9-2746

ESCALON
Cadlolo Winery
1124 California Street
838-2457

LOCKEFORD
Lockeford Winery
Locke Road
RAymond 7-5562

LODI
Coloma Cellars
368-7822

LODI (contd.)
East-Side Winery
1600 Victor Road
ENdicott 9-4768

Guild Wine Company
1 Winemaster's Way
ENdicott 8-5151

MANTECA
Delicato Vineyards
French Camp Road
982-0679

RIPON
Franzia Brothers Winery
Yosemite Avenue
599-4251

San Luis Obispo County

TEMPLETON
Pesenti Winery
Vineyard Drive
434-1030

Rotta Winery
Winery Road
434-1389

York Mountain Winery
York Mountain Road
238-3925

Santa Clara County

CUPERTINO
Ridge Vineyards*
17100 Monte Bello Rd.
867-3233

GILROY
Bertero Winery
Route 1, Box 53
VInewood 2-3032

Bonesio Winery
842-0364

Fortino Winery
Hecker Pass Highway
842-3305

Thomas Kruse Winery
Hecker Pass Highway
842-7016

Live Oaks Winery
First Street
842-2401

Rapazzini/Los Altos
Vineyards
Box 247
842-5649

LOS GATOS
Almadén Vineyards
Blossom Hill Road
ANdrews 9-1312

LOS GATOS (contd.)
David Bruce*
21439 Bear Creek Road
354-4214

Novitiate Wines
College Avenue
354-6471

MORGAN HILL
E. Guglielmo Winery
East Main Avenue
779-3064

Pedrizetti Winery
San Pedro Avenue
779-4512

Richert & Sons, Inc.
1840 W. Edmundson Ave.
779-9032

MOUNTAIN VIEW
Gemello Winery
2003 El Camino Real
WHitecliff 8-7723

SAN JOSE
Mirassou Vineyards
Route 3, Box 344
274-4000

* By appointment only.

Santa Clara County (contd.)

SAN MARTIN
San Martin Vineyards
Company
P. O. Box 53
MUtual 3-2672

SARATOGA
Paul Masson Vineyards
13150 Saratoga Avenue
257-7800

Santa Cruz County

SOQUEL
Nicasio Vineyards*
Nicasio Way
GArden 3-1073

Bargetto's Santa Cruz Winery
3535 N. Main Street
475-2258

WATSONVILLE
S. Martinelli & Company
P.O. Box 549, 227 Third Street
724-1126

Solano County

FAIRFIELD
Cadenasso Winery
Box 22
HArrison 5-5845

SUISUN CITY
Wooden Valley Winery
Route 1, Box 124
HArrison 5-3962

Sonoma County

ASTI
Italian Swiss Colony
P. O. Box 1
TWinbrook 4-2541

CLOVERDALE
Bandiera Wines
155 Cherry Creek· Road
TWinbrook 4-5887

FORESTVILLE
Russian River Vineyards
5700 Gravenstein Highway N.
887-2243

GEYSERVILLE
J. Pedroncelli Winery
1220 Canyon Road
857-3619

* By appointment only.

Sonoma County (contd.)

GEYSERVILLE (contd.)
Souverain of Alexander
Valley
Independence Lane
857-3789

Trentadue Winery
19170 Redwood Highway
433-3104

GLEN ELLEN
Grand Cru Vineyards
996-8100

GUERNEVILLE
Korbel Winery
Korbel Station
887-2294

HEALDSBURG
Cambiaso Winery
1141 Grant Avenue
433-5508

L. Foppiano Wine Company
P. O. Box 606
433-1937

Simi Winery Inc.
Healdsburg Avenue
433-4276

KENWOOD
Kenwood Vineyards
833-5891

SANTA ROSA
Martini & Prati Wines, Inc.
2191 Laguna Road
VAlley 3-2404

SONOMA
Buena Vista Vineyards
Old Winery Road
WEbster 8-8504

Hacienda Wine Cellars
1000 Vineyard Lane
938-3220

Samuele Sebastiani
388 Fourth Street
WEbster 8-5532

WINDSOR
Sonoma Vineyards
Old Redwood Highway
433-5545

Stanislaus County

SALIDA
Pirrone Wine Cellars
U.S. Route 99
545-0704

Tulare County

CUTLER
   California Growers Wineries
   P. O. Box 38
   LAwrence 8-3055

Tuolumne County

SONORA
   Butler Winery
   Rt. 3, Box 357
   586-4384

Index

INDEX

The page numbers in this index locate the place in the book where the reader can find the primary discussion of a winery or wine. Brand names, which are printed in *italics*, appear only in those cases where they are different from the names of the wineries which produce them.